■SCHOLASTIC

Poetry Lessons

EVERYTHING YOU NEED

A Mentor Teacher's Lessons and Select Poems That
Help You Meet the Standards Across the Curriculum
—and Teach Poetry with Confidence and Joy

KATHY A. PERFECT

New York • Toronto • London • Auckland • Sydney
Mexico City • New Delhi • Hong Kong • Buenos Aires

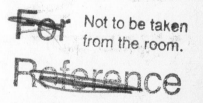

Dedication

To the Giver of all gifts—thought, desire, opportunity, talent
and hope—Who fashioned the circumstances of this book
and guided the process each step of the way, and is the true
Author of every word I wrote.

Acknowledgments

Sincere thanks to Wendy Murray whose invitation to write what
I know and love about poetry made a dream come true.

My profound gratitude to Joanna Davis-Swing—
editor extraordinaire—whose gentle spirit, keen insight, and
generous enthusiasm underscored every phase of this manuscript.
Your way with words (and anxious writers) is superb.

Gentle thanks to my students, the young poets and poetry lovers
who inspired me and made this book come alive.

Heartfelt thanks to my family and friends whose loving support
and encouragement blessed me and brought my hands back to
the keyboard time and time again.

Deepest gratitude to my husband Bill, my biggest blessing of all,
who never—not once—complained about the countless hours it
took to bring this book into the world, and whose love and
belief in me sustains me every day, no matter what.

Cover and interior design by Maria Lilja
Cover photograph © Photodisc Blue/Getty Images

ISBN: 0-439-49157-6

2 3 4 5 6 7 8 9 10   40   11 10 09 08 07 06 05

Table of Contents

Prologue

> *When you send poems out into the world,*
> *you have no idea what friends they might find.*
>
> ~ Naomi Shihab Nye

I t's the day before Christmas vacation. The kids are high with anticipation, and I'm low on energy. They're thinking of all they'll *get* to do, while I'm thinking of all I *have* to do. I have just said good-bye to my class of fourth graders, their predictable "See you next year!" responses still ringing in the hallway. My desktop is clean, my book bag packed and waiting, the lights already turned off. I grab my coat, sling my book bag over one shoulder, my purse over the other, and make my way to the office to wish anyone still around a happy holiday. It is then that I notice something in my mailbox cubby, a piece of holiday wrapping paper folded in half, with a blue bow stuck in the upper right corner. Inside, a bold headline has been photocopied at the top: *You Have a Great Gift!* Below it is a handwritten note from a former student who moved on to our district's middle school. Her message has been carefully printed in alternating green and red letters.

> *Dear Mrs. Perfect,*
>   *You have a great gift for teaching poetry. At first I didn't*
> *care for it, but now I do. You taught me how to love it.*
> *Love, Vanessa Carter*
> *Merry Christmas!*

It takes me only a few seconds to scan this note from beginning to end. I read it again, savoring every red and green word, picturing Vanessa bending over the paper with felt-tipped markers spelling out her message. I think: *You can't possibly know, Vanessa, how much your note means to me. And what a gift it is to receive it.* Such an unexpected gift.

I think of how this gift came to be. I think of the dozens—no, *hundreds!*—of poems we'd shared when Vanessa was one of my students. I think of the poems that made us laugh and others that made us sad. I remember some that confused us, some that comforted, and some that called us to go deeper into ourselves. There were those we couldn't stop talking about, while some were surrounded with silence. We may have started with Silverstein, but we also dabbled in Shakespeare, Sandburg, and Frost. I think of the way each poem touched us. One by one they left their fingerprints all over us. We will never be the same.

Vanessa claims I taught her how to love poetry. I'll take the compliment and treasure it, but in my heart I know the truth. You can't *teach* students to love poetry. You can bring poetry to them, surround them with it, immerse them in it. You can place them in the presence of poetry again and again, allowing it to weave its luminous thread in and out, back and forth, so gently you do not know at which moment it becomes the fabric that wraps each day—you only know it does. Poetry comes in like silk and wears like denim.

So I thank you, Vanessa, for your gift. But while I'm at it, maybe I should pass along this gratitude—yours *and* mine—to those who've really earned it: to Arnold Adoff, Countee Cullen, Karla Kuskin, and Naomi Shihab Nye, whose very names ring like poetry in the air. And thanks to John Ciardi, Frank Asch, Cynthia Rylant, Janet Wong, and Langston Hughes. I can't leave out Eve Merriam, Mary O'Neill, William Carlos Williams, or Myra Cohn Livingston. Thank you, Maxine Kumin, Eloise Greenfield, Stanley Kunitz, Gary Soto, Ted Hughes, and Jack Prelutsky. A very special thanks to Ogden Nash for what may have been the shortest poem on record "Fleas" ("Adam had 'em!"), until Paul Janeczko wrote "August Ice-Cream Cone Poem": "Lick quick!" Our thanks must include Judith Viorst, Sara Holbrook, and Lee Bennett Hopkins. Maya Angelou. Mary Oliver. Gwendolyn Brooks. William Stafford. e.e. cummings. Sara Henderson Hay. Yikes! It's impossible to mention and thank all the wonderful poets whose work has graced our days. So, Billy Collins, Alice Schertle, and Liz Rosenberg?—and countless others who go unnamed but not unloved?—you're in our thoughts. We thank you. Your gifts have been graciously and gratefully received. And loved.

ACCEPTING THE GIFT

All of us can have the gift of poetry. Most of us have encountered it countless times in countless ways our whole lives. Whether you already recognize poetry's appeal, have forgotten the pleasure it once brought you, or haven't yet discovered the joy it can bring, consider this book an invitation. I invite you to accept the gift, open it, and examine its features and hidden treasures. Bring it into your classroom. Create a place where your students are in the presence of poetry. In doing so, you may come to realize poetry's potential to enhance and even transform your teaching.

Recapturing the Joy of Poetry

> *Let the beauty we love be what we do.*
> *There are hundreds of ways to kneel and kiss the ground.*
>
> ~ Rumi, a Sufi poet

Poetry is part of our life experience virtually from the time we are born. It has been with us, in one form or another, ever since. Our affinity for rhyme and rhythm quite possibly begins with the sound of our very own heartbeat! Indeed, every breath we take confirms the primacy of rhythm in our lives. Even when only a few months old, babies visibly and audibly respond to rhyme and rhythm by bouncing, babbling, kicking, and clapping. Poetry's place in our lives begins with lullabies, songs, and finger games; builds to simple prayers and nursery rhymes; then advances to ever more diverse forms and types as we go through adolescence and into adulthood. Think of your own experience with poetry and how it was present in your life from the time you were very young.

Remember listening to nursery rhymes?

Little Miss Muffet sat on a tuffet and *Jack Sprat could eat no fat.*

Or hand and finger songs?

The eensy weensy spider went up the waterspout.

There were simple prayers:

Now I lay me down to sleep, I pray the Lord my soul to keep.

And early childhood songs:

I'm a little teapot, short and stout. / Here is my handle, here is my spout.

Some of my own favorite memories are of the neighborhood and playground where we called to each other in verse:

Red Rover, Red Rover, let Sally come over!

We jumped rope while chanting

> *Last night, or the night before,*
> *Twenty-four robbers came knocking at my door.*

We decided who was "it" by tapping our fists in rotation as we recited

> *One potato, two potato, three potato, four,*
> *Five potato, six potato, seven potato, more.*

We wrote verse in autograph books to declare our friendship:

> *Tell me fast / Before I faint. / Is we friends / Or is we ain't?*

Or to illustrate our cleverness:

> *Can't think. / Brain dumb. / Inspiration / Won't come. / Bad ink. /*
> *Worse pen. / Best wishes, / Amen.*

We taunted siblings or classmates with such verse as:

> *Made you look, you dirty crook.*
> *Stole your mother's pocketbook.*
> *Turned it in, turned it out,*
> *Turned it into sauerkraut.*

There were Burma Shave signs that punctuated boring road trips with welcome relief:

> *No lady likes*
> *To dance*
> *Or dine*
> *Accompanied by*
> *A porcupine.*
>
> > *—Burma Shave*

Think of all the lessons we learned more easily because they rhyme:

> *A stitch in time saves nine* and *Haste makes waste.*

Don't forget spelling hints like

> *"I" before "e" except after "c."*

And would 5- and 6-year-olds be as successful memorizing a 26-letter alphabet without those convenient little rhyming segments occurring in just the right places? I still recite this poem in my head to remember the number of days in a certain month:

Thirty days hath September,
April, June, and November.
All the rest have thirty-one
Except for February with twenty-eight alone.

But familiarity with rhyme and rhythm extends well beyond the world of childhood. It is meant for all of us, at every age, in every era. When we turn on any radio or TV, we are greeted by verse in the form of catchy slogans, advertising jingles, and all manner of rhyme and rhythm put to music—rock, rap, country, pop, and hip-hop. We see it on billboards and find it in magazines and newspapers. Greeting cards use verse to convey just the right sentiment—from irreverent humor to heartfelt devotion—for almost any occasion. Poetry even travels through cyberspace, thanks to the numerous poetry sites on the Internet. Poetry of one type or another is found nearly everywhere: in our homes, in our schools, in our neighborhoods, and in our culture. In these private and public worlds, we regularly encounter poetry and respond to it in a positive and sometimes even passionate way.

SO WHAT'S THE BAD NEWS?

If poetry is ubiquitous, a faithful companion from infancy into adulthood, with widespread appeal and applicability, why is poetry, or at least enthusiasm for it, so often missing from our classrooms? Why does our comfort level with poetry suffer when we leave our personal world and step into our professional one? Why is poetry, as Gregory Denman (1988) suggested, "the most neglected component in the language arts curriculum?" And why, according to Amy McClure (1990), do many children view poetry as the "literary equivalent of liver"? Discussions with colleagues and my own research underscore several factors contributing to poetry's absence or avoidance in the classroom (Perfect, 1999). See if you identify with any of them.

Some teachers, uncertain about method or knowledge, express fear and anxiety about teaching poetry "right." Lack of confidence in understanding poetry's literary features or in how to provide proper instruction causes some teachers to avoid it altogether. Teachers concerned with accountability, achievement testing, and the emphasis on teaching specific reading skills are unsure of poetry's place within that framework. Still others became discouraged by poetry years ago, when they were students themselves and their school experiences did precious little to foster enjoyment of it. Often the exact opposite occurred. Memories of those experiences include the following: a teacher's dull presentation or lack of enthusiasm for poetry; a focus on rhyme scheme and other poetic devices considered tedious and pointless; an emphasis on figurative language and obscure references that were difficult to understand; and a requirement to memorize poems usually without purpose and sometimes as punishment. Sadly, this legacy of poor teaching methods and attitudes has left some teachers with no effective teaching models to emulate in their own classrooms. Since they couldn't kill the messenger, they killed the message—in this case, poetry.

One last concern bears mention. The biggest complaint by far from both teachers and students involves the issue of interpretation and overanalysis. Students resent the implication that a poem has one correct meaning (usually imposed on them by the teacher), and teachers feel the burden and unease of having to provide it. Likewise, the method of analyzing a poem to get at its meaning by tearing it apart, word by word or line by line, can tear the heart right out of the poem. Nearly one hundred years ago, in *Teaching Poetry in the Grades*, Haliburton and Smith wrote this about the essence of poetry:

> The first appeal of a true poem is never to the mind, but to the soul, and it is thus that every true poem should be taught. . . . Overanalysis to discover the exact thought may prove. . . fatal to a pupil's love of a good poem.

According to many colleagues and students, this is as true today as it was in 1911. But since understanding a poem promotes enjoyment of it, it's not surprising that confusion over meaning and *ownership of meaning*—and the best way to derive it—is a dilemma for many teachers. Happily, the solution to this and other issues is not out of reach.

SO HERE'S THE GOOD NEWS!

If you can relate to any of these concerns, or have some private ones of your own, I have reassuring words to offer. Help—and hope—is on the way. In fact, you're holding it in your hands this very moment! This book was written to champion the cause of poetry in the hearts of teachers and students everywhere. Poetry is for everyone. And the *joy* of poetry is for everyone.

If you are unsure, afraid, or lack confidence, this book will serve to offer encouragement and support, and to scaffold your instruction as your confidence grows. If your natural affinity for poetry has become lukewarm or has shifted to avoidance, indifference, or disdain—for whatever reason—the account of my experiences with poetry in real classrooms with real kids could revive your own interest. Some of you may not need much convincing; you might already be mindful of poetry's place in your instruction and would appreciate fresh ideas to invigorate current teaching practices. Whatever your mindset or your students' grade level, this book can meet you there and guide you in exploring the world of poetry, a place that is both promising and satisfying.

Consider this book a resource that offers ways to use poetry to strengthen your language arts program and to reinforce literacy standards across the curriculum. Engaging in these activities and your own adaptations of them will help you reclaim your fondness for the genre of poetry and pass on to your students a legacy of celebrating poetry as you experience it together. It is my hope that you will give poetry a chance to revitalize and fortify your teaching.

WHAT YOU'LL FIND HERE (AND WHAT YOU WON'T)

This book does *not* intend to make you a poetry expert or turn your students into little poets. You do not have to recognize iambic pentameter or expect students to write odes and sonnets. This book *will*, however, help you become more familiar with poetry's unique characteristics and become more comfortable exploring the genre. It will also offer ideas to improve students' thinking, writing, and related literacy skills. This book is meant to be a practical text to use in planning lessons while helping you and your students discover poetry's allure.

With that purpose in mind, I have included many examples of poems, anecdotes, activities, discussions, and extension suggestions. The use of sidebars and boxes is designed to offer easy-to-read lists, hints, and how-tos. The glossary provides definitions and examples of poetry's features along with related terms to support your instruction and boost your confidence. The appendix contains samples of writing formats, models, and prompts; activity sheets; project instructions and guidelines; and original student poetry and related work. The bibliography lists some (though certainly not all!) of the wonderful poetry volumes I own or have used with my students and that I recommend you try in your own classroom. My hope was to make this an inclusive and versatile book, adaptable to a wide range of ages and ability levels.

TAKING THE PLUNGE

Trying out new ideas is a lot like swimming: you stand ready to enter the pool, wondering if the shallow end or the deep end is best for you. Whether you're the kind of swimmer who enters the water slowly, one careful toe at a time, or the type that dives in, this book will help you "get wet" in poetry in whatever way you're most comfortable. The end result is my aim: that you will immerse yourself in this wonderful genre and discover, or rediscover, the magic in store for you and your students. So come in. Splash around. Have fun. Poetry is waiting for you.

CHAPTER ONE

The Why, When, and How of Using Poetry in the Classroom:

Strategies for Finding Your Own Comfort Level with Teaching Poetry

Notes on the Art of Poetry

*I could never have dreamt that there were such goings-on
in the world between the covers of books,
such sandstorms and ice blasts of words,
such staggering peace, such enormous laughter,
such and so many blinding bright lights,
splashing all over the pages
in a million bits and pieces
all of which were words, words, words,
and each of which were alive forever
in its own delight and glory and oddity and light.*

~ Dylan Thomas

I'm one of those people who was born loving words—the sound of them, the feel of them on my tongue, and the power they hold to convey any thought or emotion. So how did this love of words land me in this spot—writing a book that celebrates poetry? As an avid reader of all literature, I am equally passionate about many different genres, so why choose poetry instead of another?

Poetry has a powerful magnetic pull for a word fan like myself. The language of poetry is particularly rich, distilled, concise, and carefully wrought. The poet is truly a "wordsmith" above all else. Often the words of a poem have multiple layers of meaning, layers that are mystifying and satisfying all at once. Sometimes I barely finish sharing a poem with my students before they say, "Read it again!" They seem to know intuitively that a first reading is a mere invitation to a second or third, that there's always more to "get" with every recitation. Or is their request simply a result of the joy they experience upon hearing a well-crafted poem, a little "ear candy"—as J. Patrick Lewis calls it (quoted in Fletcher, 2002)—to sweeten the day? Poetry entices students to become word lovers, too.

But aside from inviting you to explore how poetry can ignite interest in words, I had another reason for writing this book. I'm reminded of a story about a mother with many children. When asked if she had any favorites, she didn't hesitate to answer: "Yes. The one who is sick, until they are well; the one who is lost, until they are found." In a similar way, I'm a parent who loves all her "literary children" for their own unique traits, but there are times when one of them requires extra care and attention. Poetry's a dear and lovely child, but she is often overlooked, either a little or a lot. Spend time with her and get to know her. You too will be captivated by the language she speaks.

CREATING A PLACE FOR POETRY: IDEAS FOR GETTING STARTED

As with any personal relationship, the one you develop with poetry will be characterized by ideas and adaptations of your own, but perhaps my thoughts about why, when, and how to use poetry will give you a place to begin. These ideas have evolved over many years of teaching, adjusting this, discarding that, while trying to stay open to new possibilities or demands. I offer them here to provide a foundation and a rationale—just in case you need one!

Why Use Poetry?

For those who are intrigued by words and want their students to appreciate them also, poetry is the perfect genre for providing unlimited examples of rich language, creative imagery, and stimulating ideas. It captures both the imagination and the intellect. But the "word appeal" uniquely found in poetry is only one of its purposes in the classroom. Currently, most teachers are mindful of the need to teach in ways that enable our students to meet academic standards that specify what all students should know and be able to do at each grade level. English Language Arts standards were first formulated by NCTE (National Council of Teachers of English) and IRA (International Reading Association) and have provided a useful model for individual states to consult in creating their own. With these standards as a framework for instruction, many teachers use a wide variety of methods and materials to help students achieve a high level of progress. A good dose of innovation doesn't hurt. Poetry in its many forms can be used across the curriculum to enrich other academic areas as well. Each chapter of this book will offer specific techniques to use poetry in ways that matter and ways that count.

The answer to "why use poetry?" is multidimensional. Developing a love of words and meeting academic standards are only two ends of a broad spectrum. I've used poetry, for example, to show differing points of view about a topic, demonstrating to students that each of us has a perspective that is influenced by our position in life, our age, our experience, and our gender. Because poetry so often expresses the emotions, it has been the perfect genre to help students make sense of important events in their lives, such as death, divorce, friendship issues, family concerns, and even terrorism. The range of poetry available today means I can put my hands on a poem about virtually any topic ("Ballad of a Boneless Chicken"?!? by Jack Prelutsky, 1984) and often pull one into a lesson that grabs attention like nothing else can. Consider, for example, how the following poem by Allan Wolf would enliven science class:

SPIT

Saliva, better known as spit;   *that helps to turn the bread to mush,*
it seems our mouths are full of it.   *assisting the esophagus*
To see your spit at work, don't spew it;   *(a muscular and lengthy tube)*
bite a bit of bread and chew it.   *in swallowing the food you've chewed.*
Your salivary glands produce   *Although some folks think spit is rude,*
saliva, a digestive juice   *your spit helps you digest your food.*

Similarly, some of the most stimulating, provocative, and revealing discussions I've had with students have taken place after sharing a particular poem. The strong emotions evoked by Countee Cullen's "Incident" was one of these:

INCIDENT

Once riding in old Baltimore   *I saw the whole of Baltimore*
Heart-filled, head-filled with glee,   *From May until December;*
I saw a Baltimorean   *Of all the things that happened there*
Keep looking straight at me.   *That's all that I remember.*

Now I was eight and very small,
And he was no whit bigger,
And so I smiled, but he poked out
His tongue, and called me "Nigger."

One student remarked, "This poem shows how one little incident can ruin your whole day (or whole time in Baltimore) because you can't stop thinking about it. It's like a splinter—it may be small, but it causes a lot of pain." Her classmates nodded in agreement; another added, "If I were a different color, I would feel sad, upset, and angry if someone treated me that way for no reason but the color of my skin. I wonder if it changed the boy's thinking about all white people." One student speculated about the poet: "If this really happened to the poets, it must have scarred him for the rest of his life. I wonder if writing poetry is like his therapy." This brief exchange is but one example of how students respond to sophisticated and sensitive poetry, and it reminded me yet again of the profound effect poetry can have on middle school students.

One year one of my language arts classes performed the famous "balcony scene" (act 2, scene 1) from *Romeo and Juliet* for other classes, each student reciting one of the 24 lines. Here are just a few of them:

> *But soft, what light through yonder window breaks?*
> *It is the east, and Juliet is the sun.*
> *Arise, fair sun, and kill the envious moon,*
> *Who is already sick and pale with grief*
> *That thou, her maid, art far more fair than she.*
> *Be not her maid, since she is envious.*

This type of poetry presentation, in which everyone participates, helps students practice performance skills such as voice inflection, volume, and expression. Some students are surprisingly dramatic in this activity. Shakespeare's words give students entry into figurative language and help students to build on previous knowledge of literary devices such as metaphor and personification. Students may not easily comprehend each Shakespearean turn of phrase, but they do come to appreciate the power of words to convey deep thought and emotion as they read the following words evoked by Romeo's tender and passionate love for Juliet:

> *See how she leans her cheek upon her hand.*
> *O, that I were a glove upon that hand,*
> *That I might touch that cheek!*

While they may not "get" all of Shakespeare's phrasing, they understand his intent—Romeo is crazy about Juliet! Most middle school students can relate to such strong feelings. Reading and reciting poetry builds knowledge of classic poets such as Shakespeare in addition to the more contemporary poets I share with them on a regular basis. We have also used certain poems as a model for writing our own versions or as a stimulus for creative response in the form of writing, art, or drama. Other chapters in this book will give additional examples of how you, too, can use poetry in practical, immediate ways.

I've shared these few examples to give you the flavor of what poetry can do for you and your students. There are many other reasons for making it part of your teaching. See if any of these appeal to you.

WORDS TO MAKE YOU SMILE

If you're looking for a poem to showcase the sound and playfulness of language with your students, here's one that will snag them all. I dare you to read this without a smile spreading across your face—or at least in your heart!

SING ME A SONG
OF TEAPOTS AND TRUMPETS

Sing me a song
of teapots and trumpets:
Trumpots and teapets
And tippets and taps,
trippers and trappers
and jelly bean wrappers
and pigs in pajamas
with zippers and snaps.

Sing me a song
of sneakers and snoopers:
Snookers and sneapers
and snappers and snacks,
snorkels and snarkles,
a seagull that gargles,
and gargoyles and gryphons
and other knickknacks.

Sing me a song
of parsnips and pickles:
and pumpkins and pears,
plumbers and mummers
and kettle drum drummers
and plum jam (yum-yum jam)
all over their chairs.

Sing me a song—
but never you mind it!
I've had enough
of this nonsense. Don't cry.
Criers and fliers
and onion ring fryers—
It's more than I want to put up with!
Good-by!

~ N. M. Bodecker

Check out the list on page 17 of reasons to use poetry; see how many of them apply to this one poem. Now find some of your own as you explore the ways poetry fits into your classroom.

Why Use Poetry?

1. Poetry demonstrates concise, rich, imaginative language.

2. Poetry's spare, uncluttered format (e.g., short lines, arranged in stanzas, surrounded by plenty of white space) is especially suited to struggling or reluctant readers, and enhances reading motivation.

3. Poetry appeals to our natural affinity for rhyme and rhythm and promotes fluency and expression in oral reading.

4. Poetry is readily available and easily accessible, with a wide range of uses and adaptations.

5. Poetry connects to virtually any and all subject/content areas.

6. Poetry stimulates and enriches class discussions.

7. Poetry creates a "mood" depending on type or style of poem shared.

8. Regular use of poetry builds familiarity with both classic and contemporary poets.

9. Poetry gives voice to one's own human experience and feelings.

10. Poetry stands as a model for student writing and expression.

11. Poetry is a natural companion to other means of artistic expression: drama, art, music.

12. Through frequent use of poetry, students experience and learn to appreciate
    • the sound of language
    • the use of language
    • the power of language
    • the love of language

When to Use Poetry

It's hard for me to imagine a day going by without poetry in my classroom. When I taught intermediate children and had a self-contained classroom, sharing poetry usually took place first thing in the morning. I pulled a poetry book out and read a poem or two… or three… and sometimes more. Teaching older students in a middle or high school setting means sharing poetry at the start of each period or frequently integrating it into various lessons. But all teachers work within various types of constraints. Daily schedules, responsibilities, and an ever burgeoning list of demands are always issues. How to find time and space for poetry in an already full instructional day is a challenge. For some of us, though, poetry is considered a vital component of daily classroom life and learning. I use poetry in two ways: (1) to give pleasure and to develop familiarity and positive associations with the genre, and (2) to achieve specific instructional objectives such as fluency or to connect to a content-area lesson.

I recommend you start by choosing a regular time to share poetry. Select a time of day (or day of the week) when sharing poetry is likely to occur without interruption. Try to be consistent and faithful about keeping this time designated for poetry reading. For me, it's first thing in the morning, or at the beginning or end each period. My students and I look forward to it as a gentle, pleasurable transition into the routine of a school day or as an enjoyable start to or end of a lesson.

A few years ago, U.S. poet laureate Billy Collins created Poetry 180, a program designed for American high school students in which a poem is read every day of the 180 days in a school year. (See Bibliography for Web site listing the 180 poems Collins selected.) The program's name also implies a turning back, a 180-degree turn back to the sharing and enjoyment of poetry. What a grand and worthwhile notion, Billy Collins!

Though Poetry 180 was designed to bring poetry into high schools, there is no reason for limiting the program to that age group. I'd love to see this idea carried out in every school, at every level, from kindergarten through college. Imagine if students in America were treated to poetry every single day of their entire school life! But you don't have to wait for such a plan to be instituted in the U.S., your state, your district, or even your particular school—you can begin with your own classroom.

Even if you don't feel comfortable sharing a poem every day, there are many ways to bring poetry into your classroom on a regular basis. Consider the following list of suggestions below.

When to Use Poetry?

1. DAILY: as an opener or closer or anytime in between, read a poem a day (or several) just for pleasure.

2. WEEKLY: plan one lesson per week using poetry or designate one day a week (e.g., Friday afternoon) as Poetry Share Day.

3. MONTHLY/QUARTERLY: include poetry in some form in your instruction; try it not only in language arts but also in math, science, social studies, etc.

4. OCCASIONALLY: build a lesson around a poem or incorporate related poetry into a lesson.

5. INTERMITTENTLY: use poetry to initiate a season, a holiday, a special celebration; commemorate an event or an anniversary (e.g., September 11, Veterans' Day).

6. AS A THEMED POETRY UNIT: when you wish to focus on a poetry type (haiku), choose a certain poet/or poets, or a topic.

7. FOR SPECIAL EVENTS: plan an event such as a "Poetry Café" in which students will wear black berets and turtlenecks and practice and perform poetry for the class and other guests.

8. DURING POETRY WEEK: plan projects and/or performances to help celebrate National Poetry Month in April.

9. TO CREATE A MOOD: this is just the thing to calm nerves, quiet tensions, add levity, soothe fears.

10. TO SEIZE TEACHABLE MOMENTS: spark interest, challenge thinking, promote class unity.

11. TO SAVE YOUR SANITY: grab a poetry book just before tearing your hair out from fatigue or frustration; also called the "Everyone Wins" technique.

12. ONCE IN A BLUE MOON: better than nothing, but keep trying till you wonder how you ever taught without it!

How often you bring poetry into your classroom will depend on your reasons for using it. My primary goals are to encourage the enjoyment of poetry and to have my students experience a wide variety of poets, styles, themes, and types. But my list of reasons for using poetry has grown as I've seen a wider application and usefulness for the genre in my overall literacy and curricular programs. In making decisions about poetry—how often, how much—ask yourself some questions:

1. What benefits could poetry provide for my students?

2. What are some ways poetry could enhance or enliven my teaching?

3. Which academic standards could I meet through the genre of poetry?

4. How can poetry fit into different areas of the curriculum?

5. How can I use poetry to make connections, deepen meaning, or extend the learning of my students?

6. Where could I find time to share a poem or two with my students?

7. Am I willing to try poetry on a regular basis—daily, weekly, monthly, or whatever feels right for me—in order to receive the benefits of poetry?

Once you include poetry in your teaching, answers to these questions will emerge naturally. Sometimes you just have to trust the poetry to work on and with students without always knowing where it will take you. Poems have a power of their own to guide you into possibilities you couldn't imagine. The more often you share poetry, the more benefits you'll recognize for your students and your instruction.

30-SECOND HUMOR BREAK

Are you ready for a little whimsy, a bit of "let's not take everything so seriously if we can help it"? Next time your class (or an individual!) is ready for a restroom break, read this Judith Viorst poem before they leave the room—but be ready for a quick exit!

DON'T THINK

Don't think rivers.
Don't think fountains.
Don't think mountain streams or creeks.
Don't think pools or ponds or oceans.
Don't think lakes and don't think leaks.
Don't think wells or wet or water.
Don't think showers.
Don't think springs.
Don't think moist or damp or rainy.
Don't think hurricanes or things
That drizzle, dribble, drip, drop, flood, or flow,
When there's no bathroom—and you gotta go.

Good. There you have it. The makings of a light-hearted moment, compliments of a poet with a sense of humor.

How to Use Poetry

Now that we've examined the why and the when of sharing poetry, we can explore the how of making poetry come alive for you and your students. This often starts in simple ways that take on added dimensions over time. Beyond the regular sharing of poetry for pleasure, you might begin by choosing an objective related to specific needs of your students or particular skills you're trying to teach. We know, for example, that there is a positive correlation between fluency—the clear, easy oral expression of written text—and reading comprehension. So if you're interested in improving oral reading fluency or reading motivation, you would use a poem geared to that purpose. Keep in mind, however, that enjoyment of the poem should always be a primary objective.

Try It Out!

USE POETRY FOR FLUENCY PRACTICE

Poetry is a highly effective way to promote fluency and motivation at the same time and is especially conducive to certain kinds of fluency practice. Give students short, manageable, and engaging text in the form of poetry; model a fluent, expressive way to read it; and then invite them to do individual or paired choral reading of it. Those of us teaching at the intermediate and middle school level need to keep this in mind—fluency is not just for primary-age students.

Virtually any poem is suitable for fluency practice, whether students read in pairs or go solo. The rhyme and rhythm of the following poem, combined with its lighthearted humor, makes it great fun to read again and again.

BROTHER

I had a little brother
And I brought him to my mother
And I said I want another
Little brother for a change.
But she said don't be a bother
So I took him to my father
And I said this little bother
Of a brother's very strange.

But he said one little brother
Is exactly like another
And every little brother
Misbehaves a bit he said.
So I took the little bother
From my mother and my father
And I put the little bother
Of a brother back to bed.

~ Mary Ann Hoberman

The following ideas for how to use poetry can be paired with ideas from the section "Why Use Poetry?" The way you combine or configure them is part of the fun in planning instruction. Some poems are perfect for fluency practice, others for teaching alliteration (Jack Prelutsky comes to mind here!), and still others for imagery. Many poems make thought-provoking discussions likely, while some provide a natural link to a topic under study. In a math lesson on understanding the value of money and the concept of subtraction, I always include the poem "Smart" by Shel Silverstein, which I hope you're familiar with. If not, I highly recommend *A Light in the Attic*, an indispensable poetry book. The first time through, read the poem to enjoy the foolish innocence of the boy telling the sequence of events in the poem; he thinks he increases his net worth by exchanging a dollar for two quarters. Then read the poem again and have students do the math calculation to see what the boy ends up with.

One of the joys you'll discover along the way is the diverse and creative application of individual poems. As you bring poetry into your classroom, it helps to have suggestions for getting started. Before long, however, you'll be adding your own great ideas to the list. Here are some other ways I've included poetry in my instruction through the years:

How to Use Poetry

1. As oral reading fluency practice through individual or choral readings or by memorizing a favorite poem to recite to others.

2. As an introduction to a lesson or concept or to extend literature/content-area topics

3. As a literary component in themed units of study; pair with other genres around a common theme or topic (fiction, nonfiction, poetry).

4. As inspiration for creative expression in students' own poetry and/or art, and as a springboard for various writing activities and other creative work.

5. As a model for individual written adaptations (e.g., Copy-Change activity; see page 70)

6. As a stimulus for dramatic interpretation (tableaux, use of props, etc.) and as a companion to music, works of art, photographs, and artifacts.

7. To identify different poetry forms (limerick, sonnet, cinquain, etc.).

8. To encourage critical thinking strategies through various activities.

9. To examine literary elements such as simile, metaphor, and point of view.

10. As the basis of comparative lessons:
    • rhyme vs. free verse
    • poetry vs. prose
    • how different poets approach the same topic

11. For individual poet studies that focus on characteristics of specific poets (for example, Jack Prelutsky's frequent use of alliteration or Emily Dickinson's style and her love of nature).

12. Plan a lesson around a poem (for example, "Smart" by Shel Silverstein to work on subtraction and money values).

Keep in mind that while you can certainly use poetry to help teach important skills and concepts, such as fluency, I highly recommend sharing poems with students on a regular basis. This simple practice establishes familiarity with poetry, creates a "comfort zone" within the genre, and serves as the foundation for future poetry experiences.

Choose a Poem

❀ to feature a certain theme, poet, style, or topic

❀ to create or reflect a mood: serious, humorous, thought-provoking, and so on

❀ in response to current events

❀ in response to the weather (frigid? read "The Cremation of Sam McGee")

❀ to answer a particular need in the classroom (friendship problems, a pet dying)

❀ to satisfy a student's request

❀ to mark an important event or the anniversary of an event (September 11: poems from *This Place I Know: Poems of Comfort*, selected by Georgia Heard)

❀ to illustrate a literary device such as simile, metaphor, or personification

❀ to enhance content-area subjects you're studying

❀ to introduce or wrap up a lesson

❀ to make connections across genres or to other books being read

❀ to experience vivid imagery, powerful word choice, alliteration, rhyme scheme, etc.

FOUR STEPS TO A SUCCESSFUL POETRY SHARE

Now we'll take a look at how to share poetry so you and your students get the most out of the experience. The following are some practical tips for how to select, introduce, share, and encourage students to respond to poetry. There are no rules for how to go about this except. . . just do it!

1. Selecting Poetry

When selecting poetry to share with your students, the first thing to remember is to be true to yourself. Some of the ideas I share will not suit your personality or style of teaching. Take and use the parts you like and leave the rest. And by all means, fiddle around with the details to make poetry sharing fit who you are, who your students are, the subject(s) you teach, and your time constraints.

To get started, buy or borrow a good poetry anthology or two, which will provide an array of poets, styles, topics, and types of poetry, as well as a wealth of individual poems that will last for many weeks or months of enjoyment. (See the bibliography for recommended books.) Over time, add more poetry books to your collection that will offer you and your students a wide spectrum of choices and possibilities. As you read through the books, flag poems that you like or that you think your students would enjoy.

One way to hook students early is to share poetry with a solid track record. To help a new class develop a positive attitude toward the genre, select poetry at first that has universal "crowd appeal," such as the humorous and sometimes silly work of Shel Silverstein and Jack Prelutsky, or poetry that's fun to hear and say by Ogden Nash, Karla Kuskin, and John Ciardi. Before long, start including poetry of all kinds: serious, lighthearted, classic, contemporary, rhyming, and free verse. Nothing needs to be off-limits except poetry with language or content that is not appropriate for the age and maturity of your students.

2. Preparing to Read

Before sharing a poem with students, give it a quick read-through—preferably out loud—to establish the rhythm of it in a comfortable, natural way. Avoid reading in a singsong voice, or being either too dull or overly dramatic (not that a fair amount of expression is a bad thing!). Your voice, cadence, and mood will be different according to the type of poem you share. The nature and brevity of haiku, for example, conveys a simple message; your voice will be soft and understated when reading it. Other poems might need a lively tone, a fast pace, and an air of intensity to accurately interpret the rhythm, meter, or subject matter. Relax and let the poems guide you along. Much as we encourage repeated readings of text with students, repeated events of sharing poetry will improve your fluency, too!

Initially, you may want to limit your sharing to a single poem as students become accustomed to both the genre and the routine (and realistically, you may have time in your schedule for only one poem). But after a while, you may find that reading a few poems at a time works out.

3. Sharing the Poem

Start your poetry share with a simple introduction: "This poem comes from (title of book) and was written by (name of poet)." You may want to give students a particular feature or poetic device to focus on, such as repetition or imagery, or briefly say something about the poem's theme: "This is a poem about (friendship or homework or falling in love)." At this point in a poetry share, I settle into my "poetry-reading mode." I pause a few seconds, straighten my posture a bit, position the book in front of me, and begin reading in a clear voice. I say the poem's title (unless it is untitled) followed by the poet's name—"'Fleas' by Ogden Nash"—then I read the poem itself. Keeping this pattern consistent (title, poet, poem) provides a model for students to use when they want to read or recite poetry to the class. We honor the poem by selecting it in the first place; we honor the poet by naming him or her when we read.

> # Give Students a Purpose for Listening
>
> When we tell students what to listen for, they know what to focus on. These advance cues support understanding and engagement:
>
> Listen for
>
> - rhythm and rhyme scheme
> - repetition of sounds, words, lines
> - voice or point of view
> - attention to sensory details
> - use of imagery
> - figurative language
> - unusual or unknown words
> - mood created by poem
> - clues about the poet from her words/style/theme

4. Guiding Response to the Poem

When you've finished reading, allow a few minutes for students to respond in whatever way seems appropriate. Resist the urge to have students analyze every poem, and don't expect them to say something profound in response to one. Often some of the most meaningful poems elicit no comments at all because *they are too compelling for words!* Or too confusing. It's okay to allow some uncertainty in our thoughts without seeking clarity or explanations. Help your students reside in ambiguity by being comfortable with it yourself. Don't be so proud that you can't admit your own confusion. Be honest if a particular poem doesn't "grab" you or speak to you. Not every poem will and not every poem needs to.

Many poetry shares result in discussion that is lively, informative, focused, and rewarding. Often, I guide students along in their thinking by posing a simple question, like "What do you think?" or "What did you notice?" Or I might engage in a "think aloud" type of commentary, such as "I wonder why the poet repeated certain words" or "The rhythm in this poem reminds me of gliding on ice skates." Allow time for students to respond with their own observations. Respect students' ideas and interpretations of a poem (within reason, of course), taking care not to impose too much of your own meaning on the encounter. As literate mentors, we are more likely to bring students to the heart of a poem through gentle guidance than through rigid insistence on one interpretation. See the box of suggested questions at the left.

Finally, consider that almost any poem is worth a second reading, especially if it contains words or sounds that are fun or challenging to say and hear. Likewise, the rich sensory images found in many poems are more fully appreciated with multiple readings. Poetry also bears repeating if it is thought-provoking or has an elusive quality to it. Be ready to respond to students who spontaneously say, "Read it again!" by granting their request. Their enthusiasm will tell you that poetry is working its magic. Rereading a poem

Try It Out!

PAIR POEMS WITH VISUAL ART

As we've seen, poetry stands perfectly fine on its own. Yet poetry can also be a wonderful companion to other literature, music, or works of art. *Heart to Heart: New Poems Inspired by Twentieth-Century American Art* (2001) is a collection of poems, each one inspired by and a companion to a particular work of art. One poem in this book, written by Jane Yolen, is paired with Grant Wood's famous oil painting *American Gothic*. While most students are familiar with this painting (and if they're not, the book includes the painting to help you out), Yolen's words compel us to look at it in a new way.

GRANT WOOD: AMERICAN GOTHIC

Do not dwell on the fork,
the brooch at the throat,
the gothic angel wing
of window pointing toward
a well-tended heaven.
Do not become
a farmer counting cows

as if the number of the herd
defines you.
Look behind the eyes,
to see who looks out at you.
We are not what we own.
We own what we would be.

In this poem, Yolen invites us to look beyond the obvious in the painting, to the person behind the eyes looking out at us. Or is she inviting the farmer in the painting to take a closer look at his wife? She may be warning us to be wise in what we value, or careful in the way we define ourselves. There are many possibilities in this thought-provoking poem, as is true for all the pairings of artwork and poetry in the book. Invite students to offer their own interpretations of both the artwork and the poems. Have them write their own companion poetry to famous artwork and share the results by displaying the pairings on a bulletin board for others to see.

leads to more enjoyment, better understanding, and heightened impact. It takes only a few seconds to do so, yet so much is gained in the process.

LOOKING AHEAD

Now that you've considered why, when, and how to use poetry, you are ready to let poetry transform your classroom. Create a place for poetry in ways that suit your needs, your style, and your curriculum. The next chapter will familiarize you with some poetry basics and various poems to use with your students as you share and discuss poetry with them.

CHAPTER TWO

The Basics and Beyond:

Creative Ways to Introduce Poems to Students—and Teach Key Poetic Elements

The poem is not the world.
It isn't even the first page of the world.
But the poem wants to flower, like a flower.
It knows that much.
It wants to open itself,
like the door of a little temple,
so that you might step inside and be cooled and refreshed,
and less yourself than part of everything.

~ Mary Oliver

In the first chapter I gave you several things to consider: reasons for using poetry, how often to bring it into your teaching, and ways to share poetry with students. In this chapter I'll discuss the essential poetic elements we expect students to know, along with lessons for introducing them. There's no one "right" way to teach poetry and no prescribed order in which to teach it; I will simply offer suggestions for lessons and sequences that have worked for me over the years.

You don't have to know a lot about poetry to enjoy it or to make it a part of your instruction. Some basic knowledge is enough for most readers, listeners, and novice writers of poetry: what is poetry, what is its purpose, and what can it do for us? There is certainly no shortage of ideas about or definitions of it. Some are simple and straightforward, others more elusive and mysterious, much like poetry itself. A good place to start is with a basic description of poetry and its characteristics. Let's take a look at what poets have to say about it.

POETS ON POETRY

How do we recognize poetry when we read or hear it? Emily Dickinson recognized it this way: "If. . . it makes my whole body so cold no fire can warm me, I know that is poetry. If I feel physically as if the top of my head were taken off, I know that is poetry" (Rosenberg, 1998). William Stafford's view may be less lyrical but no less enlightening: "A poem is anything said in such a way, or put on the page in such a way, as to invite from the hearer or reader a certain kind of attention." Erica Jong simply calls it "voice music." Let's look at what other poets say.

Carl Sandburg: "Poetry is the synthesis of hyacinths and biscuits. . . an echo asking a shadow to dance."

Robert Frost: "Poetry is when an emotion has found its thought and the thought has found words."

Rita Dove: "Poetry is language at its most distilled and most powerful."

Quincy Troupe: "Poetry is the living language of the community."

Maurya Simon: "Poetry is a kind of marriage between images and the rattle, click, or rustling of the right words moving against each other in the eye, ear, and mind."

Galway Kinnell: "Poetry is the singing of what it is to be on our planet."

Li-Young Lee: "Poetry safeguards or is that place at which we stand unknown to ourselves, yet fully revealed."

Stanley Kunitz: "Poetry is. . . the telling of stories of the soul."

Reading these poets' thoughts is much like reading poetry; there is an elusive quality to their words, like trying to grab steam rising from a teacup. We have a sense of what is meant, an essence just visible from the corner of our eye, or just on the edge of our understanding. Well, here—let this poem by Eleanor Farjeon express it:

POETRY

What is Poetry? Who knows?
Not a rose, but the scent of the rose;
Not the sky, but the light in the sky;
Not the fly, but the gleam of the fly;

Not the sea, but the sound of the sea;
Not myself, but what makes me
See, hear, and feel something that prose
Cannot: and what it is, who knows?

This poem illustrates that even a poet can find the nature of poetry complex and mysterious. In the last two lines, we read that poetry has the ability to do something that prose cannot—to communicate in a way that distinguishes it from other types of writing. Helping students learn the difference between prose and poetry is a good way of introducing the genre to them.

GETTING YOUR FEET WET: SIX LESSONS FOR THE FIRST SIX WEEKS

You might try the following sequence of lessons in the first weeks of a school year or semester to introduce students to poetry and familiarize them with the genre. While not meant to be prescriptive or definitive, this chronology is one way to help students step gradually into the world of poetry:

1. Prose vs. Poetry
2. Rhymed Verse and Free Verse
3. Repetition, Repetition, Repetition
4. Exploring the Power of Language
5. The Poet's Use of Imagery
6. Figurative Language

Lesson One: Prose vs. Poetry

It is important for students to learn to distinguish prose from poetry, not only to recognize the look of each as it's arranged on a page but also to understand the purpose and value of both types of writing. Students' experience with print, especially beyond the primary grades, comes almost exclusively in the form of **prose**. Virtually everything they read or write in their daily learning—textbooks, chapter books, directions, assignments, homework—is prose. In spite of its ubiquitous nature, however, I have found that most students are not familiar with the term *prose* to designate this commonplace form of writing. Some brief instruction is usually sufficient and helps set up the distinctions between prose and poetry.

Part One: The Basics of Prose

I begin by guiding students through a review of the types of reading and writing they do on a regular basis every day, both at school and at home. I ask them to take out a textbook, open to a certain page, and tell me what they see. Their answers focus on the typical format of most texts: chapter or section headings, paragraphs, lists, sets of questions for discussion or review, vocabulary words in bold print, and so on. Then we take a quick look at literature, the chapter books they have on hand, and discuss the arrangement of words on a page—chapter titles followed by paragraphs telling the story. Next, I ask them about their own writing: "What does your writing look like when you do assignments or homework? How do you organize it and/or arrange it on the paper?" Their responses indicate the characteristics of prose (though they rarely use the term itself) including the conventions of print. They typically say things like "We usually write in sentences that are capitalized, punctuated, and form a complete thought"; "Paragraphs have to be indented"; "We write from the left-hand margin to the right edge of the paper"; and "We use other capital letters and punctuation when needed." Finally, I ask, "What is the purpose of the reading and writing we've been looking at and talking about?" Together we establish a list: to entertain, to inform or instruct, to give directions, to tell a story, to persuade, to organize ideas, to analyze, and so on. Now that we've identified the features and purposes of prose writing, I provide the word *prose* to label it. We do a brief check in a dictionary to cap off the lesson: *prose—the ordinary form of spoken or written language; plain language not arranged in verses, especially the literary form, characterized by narration, description, and exposition, used in novels, plays, and articles.*

This kind of lesson helps students recognize the basic features of prose, and as we work to meet language arts standards, our instruction typically focuses on these prose elements: varied sentence structures, paragraphs organized around a clear main idea, sufficient supporting details, appropriate and effective vocabulary, and attention to audience and purpose. These are essential aspects of sound instructional goals. The defining characteristics of poetry, however, are seldom given attention. In a well-balanced and thorough literacy program, poetry is valued as an important literary genre, and students are guided into familiarity with its unique features just as they learn to recognize prose and other literary forms.

Part Two: The Basics of Poetry

What makes poetry different from other types of literature? After all, both prose and poetry use words to say what wants or needs to be said. There is an essential characteristic, however, that lifts poetry to a place where it stands alone, separate from other writing. Samuel Taylor Coleridge (in Winokur, 1990) explained the difference this way: "Prose—words in their best order; poetry—the best words in their best order." Well, how could a lover of words not be intrigued by such a distinction?

Among the compelling reasons for bringing this genre into the classroom is this very feature— poetry often does provide "the best words in their best order." We want our students to develop vocabularies that are rich and diverse and to write with words that will challenge their intellect as well as their creativity. We encourage the use of **figurative language**, such as **similes** and **metaphors**, and help students develop an understanding of figures of speech by citing frequent examples from all genres of literature. We ask them to be alert for words that are fun to say, interesting to hear, and inviting to learn. Through our lessons in language arts as well as other content areas, we teach with the expectation that our students will become more literate and articulate. Poetry is a great vehicle for taking us there. But if we want to travel that road, students need to feel comfortable with the genre. The next part of the lesson will serve as a road map for the journey.

Once students understand the key features of prose, I help them see how poetry differs. Poetry basics and terms can be taught all at once as a follow-up to the prose lesson, either on the same day or shortly thereafter, but I prefer discussing them in the context of sharing poetry. The experience of reading and discussing actual poems offers a graceful entry into the more technical aspects of the genre.

Rereading a Poem

Every poem is worthy of a second reading or more. Here's why:

With the first reading of a poem, a listener gain

- an overview of rhythm, rhyme, subject, and theme.

- familiarity with tone, style, and mood.

- a general, broad impression of the poem.

With the second and subsequent readings, a listener can

- experience heightened enjoyment.

- focus on the specifics of the rhyme scheme.

- listen for appealing, intriguing, or unusual words.

- listen for the use of imagery and figurative language.

- savor the sounds of words, phrases, and repetition.

- increase understanding and derive deeper meaning.

- commit certain words and phrases to memory.

- practice reading or listening skills.

- improve fluency (and thus comprehension).

As I share various poems with students over the next week or so, I begin to draw attention to the unique characteristics of poetry such as rhyme, rhythm, line breaks, meter, and so on. I introduce these concepts individually or a few at a time, depending on how well a particular poem exhibits a certain feature. This direct instruction of key terms helps establish a common vocabulary that will facilitate our discussions of poetry throughout the year. Once this foundation is set early on and students become familiar with the nature of poetry and confident working within the genre, I continue to add other poetry terms and concepts along the way. The following discussion offers key concepts you will want to cover with your own students early in the year. (The Glossary includes a more comprehensive list of terms and definitions.) Because there are virtually countless poems that could illustrate these features, feel free to try the poems I suggest here or use your own judgment and preference to select poems that demonstrate rhyme, rhythm, alliteration, and so forth.

Typically, poetry is thought of as an arrangement of words in **lines** of varying lengths (usually much shorter than lines of prose) that have a particular **rhythm**, sometimes called **meter**, and often include a **rhyme scheme**. Rhythm is one of the key hallmarks of poetry; it is the regular repetition of a beat, an accent, the rise and fall of syllables (stressed and unstressed), and the arrangement of these from word to word and line to line. It is a kind of cadence, a repetitive and measured march, walk, or waltz through the lines of the poem. Rhythm is felt in our physical being, much like our heartbeat can be felt in our pulse. A poem's rhythm makes us want to tap, clap, or sway as we read it, the way we might with these lines from "Eldorado" by Edgar Allan Poe:

from ELDORADO

Gaily bedight,
A gallant knight,
In sunshine and in shadow,
Had journeyed long,
Singing a song,
In search of Eldorado.

The rhythm in this example contributes to the pleasure we experience as we visualize the knight, on horseback, galloping along on his journey. We "go along for the ride" as we feel the rhythm of the words. Since rhythm is such a quintessential trait of poetry, you will easily find other poetry to help students appreciate the effect.

Rhyme scheme in poetry, a frequent companion to rhythm, is a planned, deliberate pattern of rhyming words. Repetition of sounds at the end of lines produces **end-rhyme poetry**. I show students how to indicate rhyme scheme in poetry—by using the same lowercase letter of the alphabet for all lines rhyming with each other—with an example or two. In this manner, the rhyme scheme of "Eldorado" would be designated as *aabccb*. The rhyme scheme of limericks, a five-line poem often noted for its irreverence and humor, is one of its identifying features. It follows an *aabba* rhyme pattern, which can be seen in the following example:

There once was a man from Blackheath	**a**
Who sat on his set of false teeth.	**a**
He cried with a start,	**b**
"Oh, Lord, bless my heart!	**b**
I've bitten myself underneath!"	**a**

Determining rhyme scheme is an easy and enjoyable way for students to examine rhyming patterns and the careful, clever, or playful words poets choose for their work. After doing a few poems together, students are quite capable of finding the rhyme scheme of other poems on their own.

In order to appreciate certain features of poetry, such as rhyme scheme, lines, line breaks, and stanzas, students need not only to hear poetry, but also to see poetry on the page—lots and lots of it. Students can see at a glance that the **lines** of most poems are much shorter than the lines in prose. Examining **line length** involves more than counting how few or how many words there are in a line, however. I want students to learn that line length helps a poet achieve a desired rhyming pattern or create a certain emphasis or rhythm with the words of a poem. Line length directly determines another feature of poetry—the **line break**—the place where a line of poetry ends. It is here that the reader pauses briefly, sometimes imperceptibly so, or takes a longer breath, then moves on to the next line of the poem. I share this poem by William Carlos Williams to show that lines in poetry can be quite short, and a line break can occur after only one word:

THE RED WHEELBARROW

so much depends
upon

a red wheel
barrow

glazed with rain
water

beside the white
chickens

Together we identify the pattern of words in the lines of this poem: three words, one word, three words, one word, and so on. As I share poetry on a regular basis with my students, noticing line length and line breaks becomes almost second nature to us. In a particular poem, if these features stand out or are significant in some way, I draw attention to them. Otherwise, they simply exist as a natural part of the landscape of poetry.

Another feature that sets poetry apart from prose is the arrangement of lines, especially in rhymed poetry, into groups or sets. This grouping of lines is called a **stanza**. Typically composed of two to six lines, stanzas are often separated by a space to make a poem easier to read, and/or to organize the lines into "sets" according to the rhyme scheme. The visual organization of stanzas in poetry can be compared loosely to the way prose is written in paragraphs. When I share the following poem by Robert Frost with my students, we notice it is arranged in four-line stanzas called **quatrains**, which adds another poetry term to their repertoire. I also use this poem to reinforce the practice of identifying rhyme scheme.

DUST OF SNOW

The way a crow   (Rhyme scheme: *abab cdcd*)
Shook down on me
The dust of snow
From a hemlock tree

Has given my heart   (Two four-line stanzas)
A change of mood
And saved some part
Of a day I had rued.

Seeing poems arranged in stanzas—a common occurrence in rhyming poetry—helps to familiarize students with this feature, which they begin to notice more readily with each new poem they see.

Lesson Two: Rhymed Verse and Free Verse

What about the different forms of poetry? By now, most of us are familiar with the traditional **rhyming poetry**, or **end-rhyme poetry**, as found in "Dust of Snow" by Robert Frost. We may, however, be a bit uncertain about the other major category of poetry. Much contemporary poetry is written in "open form," or **free verse**—poetry that avoids regular meter and rhyme schemes. In other words, free verse is less rigid or constrained than typical rhyming poetry in terms of line length and meter yet may still employ rhyme as one of its features. Robert Frost (in Winokur, 1990), clearly not a fan of the form, once likened writing free verse to "playing tennis with the net down." Free verse, however, does not mean "free for all" or "anything goes." The poet of free verse, though free of some of the constraints of those who write end-rhyme poetry, must be

Focus on Features of Poetry

To reinforce various literary and poetic devices, point them out as you share poems that exhibit those features. This builds confidence and increases knowledge of the genre, and enhances appreciation for the poet's craft.

FEATURES TO MENTION:

* rhyme scheme or pattern
* rhythm
* repetition
* stanzas
* line breaks
* alliteration
* imagery
* figurative language (metaphor, simile, personification)
* rhymed poetry or free verse
* mood or tone
* theme

BEFORE READING A POEM, direct attention to various features in this way:

* "Here's a poem with an *abcb* rhyme scheme."
* "This free verse poem includes repetition that adds to the rhythm of it."
* "The rhythm of this poem makes me feel like I'm floating (running, skipping, galloping . . .)."
* "Listen for any words in this poem that are interesting or unfamiliar to you."
* "Visualize the images the poem creates as you listen to it."

AFTER READING OR REREADING, ask questions about certain features to guide understanding:

* "Did you hear any examples of repetition (alliteration, etc.)?"

* "Which of your senses did this poem appeal to, and what words or phrases contributed to that?"
* "Name the metaphor or simile (or other figure of speech) in this poem."
* "How effective are the line breaks in this poem? What is their impact?"
* "What is the rhyme scheme used in this poem?"
* "How does this poem make you feel? What is its tone, mood, or theme?"
* "Is this written in free verse, or end-rhyme? What rhythm do you feel?"

equally attentive to word choice and phrasing. Both free verse and rhymed poetry include elements of rhythm, imagery, and concise, imaginative language. Since free verse and rhymed poetry seem to share several traits while being very different in others, some direct instruction often clears up any confusion students may have with these two major categories of poetry, and that is where I turn my attention once we've had an overview of the basics.

In lesson one, I help students see the difference between poetry and prose. Once they have a general sense of the distinction, and I've introduced some of the key characteristics of poetry that set it apart from prose, I know they're on their way to understanding these basics. At this point I move into a discussion of rhymed verse and free verse, which illustrates the concepts and reinforces the idea that not all poetry has to rhyme, an important point I want students to realize early on.

Understanding the difference between the two common poetry types—rhymed poetry and free verse—helps students gain confidence with poetry in general. Direct instruction in these categories of poetry is not overly involved or difficult and can be accomplished with simple examples of both types. I sometimes use the following poems with students to illustrate the distinctions between rhymed verse and free verse. To start out, I might say, "Both of these poems express thoughts about rain, each in their own way. Listen as I read each one, and think about what differences you notice." As we read them, I help students notice the features of rhyme and rhythm, the length of lines, and the variation in free verse compared to the more patterned conventions of rhymed verse.

Rhymed Verse:	*Free Verse:*
RAIN POEM	**APRIL RAIN SONG**
The rain was like a little mouse,	Let the rain kiss you.
quiet, small and gray.	Let the rain beat upon your head with
It pattered all around the house	silver liquid drops.
and then it went away.	Let the rain sing you a lullaby.
	The rain makes still pools on the sidewalk.
It did not come, I understand,	The rain makes running pools in the gutter.
indoors at all, until	The rain plays a little sleep-song on our
it found an open window and	roof at night.
left tracks upon the sill.	And I love the rain.
—Elizabeth Coatsworth	—Langston Hughes

We discuss "Rain Poem" first. It has an obvious rhyme scheme and a consistency in the rhythm and line length. I read the poem aloud once or twice to feel the rhythm within it. I take care not to overemphasize the rhythm; instead, I let the gentle flow of it occur naturally as I read. I ask my students, "Which words or lines rhyme in this poem?" Together we locate the rhyming words and the lines in which they are found to determine the poet's rhyme scheme. I guide them to see that

Coatsworth's poem has an *abab/cdcd* rhyme scheme. This leads us to notice that the poem is arranged in two four-line stanzas; I remind them that these are called **quatrains**. My students like to read the poem alone or in pairs, either in unison or alternating lines or stanzas, several times. Our sharing, discussion, and oral/choral reading has taken less than ten minutes. Once students see this as an example of end-rhyme poetry, there is no need to overanalyze or extend this poem. Rather, I want enjoyment of this simple rhyming poem to be their lasting impression of it.

After we've read and enjoyed "Rain Poem," I immediately introduce "April Rain Song," a free verse poem in which the line length is varied and there is no rhyme pattern. The poet does, however, use repetition of words and phrases to achieve a rhythm and flow. I read the poem aloud once and then again to establish a rhythm with the words. I am careful to note there is no end rhyme present in this poem. Then I ask students, "Which words and phrases are repeated? How often?" We notice that the first three lines all begin the same, with: "Let the rain," and the next three lines continue that repetitive pattern, with: "The rain." This discussion focuses the students' attention on the difference between rhymed and free verse poetry, and the presence of rhythm in both.

Students enjoy reciting this poem several times on their own or in a small group, with each person saying a line and all joining in on the last. Each time we read it aloud, the repetitive nature of the words reinforces in our mind and senses the feel, sound, and look of rain as it steadily falls to earth.

Recognizing the distinctions between rhymed poetry and free verse will enable you and your students to identify further examples. Sometimes, lack of familiarity with free verse is a factor in students' preference for the more traditional format of rhyming poetry. Frequent exposure to poetry of all kinds will serve to expand their outlook. Generally speaking, most contemporary poetry is written in free verse and most of classic poetry is end-rhymed. Together with your students you will come to appreciate both styles of poetry not only for their uniqueness but also for their similarities. As characterized in "April Rain Song" above, one of these similarities is the use of repetition. We examine this particular element more closely in the next lesson.

Lesson Three: Repetition, Repetition, Repetition

Once students grasp the difference between free verse and rhymed verse, I find that they're ready for a lesson on repetition, since this feature occurs in both types of poetry. Repetition of exact words, phrases, or lines is commonly found in poetry of all kinds. The use of rhyming patterns or **alliteration** are other ways of achieving repetition within a poem. (Poets use these devices in their work to create various impressions on the reader, and I like to introduce these elements early in the year.) The next lesson is one I've used to teach these important concepts.

The following poem by Mary Ann Hoberman is an excellent example of how repetition contributes to rhyme and rhythm in poetry.

MAY FLY

Think how fast a year flies by
A month flies by
A week flies by
Think how fast a day flies by
A May fly's life lasts but a day
A single day
To live and die
A single day
How fast it goes

The day
The May fly
Both of those.
A May fly flies a single day
The daylight dies and darkness grows
A single day
How fast it flies
A May fly's life
How fast it goes.

This is a poem that begs to be read—aloud, of course, and more than once. At first reading, the repetition of certain words and alliterative quality of this poem give it the feel of a tongue twister, but on subsequent readings, the poignancy behind the words reveals itself.

The first time I read this poem, I ask students just to listen to the feel of the words, the presence of repetition, and the rhythm. Before reading it again, I draw attention to the repeated words (*fly, flies, day,* etc.) by saying, "This time, listen for the poet's use of repetition. Notice which words are repeated." Next, I hand out copies of the poem to each student, and together we count how many times a particular word is repeated and note the variations that occur (*fly, flies, fly's*). "You'll notice," I say, "these variations are the singular, plural, and possessive forms of the word *fly*."

At this point, I want to help students appreciate the craft of poetry and the skill that goes into writing a poem. To do this, I point out the care this poet took in devising such a pattern: "Hoberman uses essentially the same words—but not quite. They differ in spelling and meaning (e.g., *fly* as both a noun and a verb) and were selected intentionally, precisely, and with great effect to give the poem its overall rhythm." Then we look at the brief line length throughout the poem. Students often remark this way: "Most of the lines are very short so we can read them quickly." I lead students to recognize this element as yet another conscious choice the poet makes by saying, "It's no accident that the brief lines in this poem suggest the short life span of a May fly. The poet had to consider such things as she wrote." Through this discussion, we've discovered how careful, skillful choices add to both rhythm and meaning, yet I am mindful that this is a poem to be savored for its sounds and its content, not to be overanalyzed or picked apart. The best part comes as we read or listen to the poem again and again to help us appreciate both the words and the meaning behind them. The repetition *in* the poem and *of* the poem contributes to our enjoyment.

This one poem shows us several examples of how repetition can occur in the form: by repeating exact words; by establishing a pattern of rhyming words; and by using alliteration and rhythm. I like to point out to students that repetition in poetry has an effect on the reader or listener—sometimes subtle, sometimes forceful—that increases pleasure and promotes understanding of the poem. Since repetition is so frequently used, you and your students will encounter this common characteristic regularly as you experience other poems. It is meant to be noticed; it is a purposeful element used with care by the poet. It is also one students pick up on easily, giving them confidence when they approach a new poem.

Lesson Four: Exploring the Power of Language

Over the first few weeks, we've covered a lot of ground in our efforts to understand the fundamentals of poetry. Students carry with them all the discussion we've had about the basics, concepts that have been examined, experienced, and reinforced a number of times in these early days. It makes sense to also take some time to focus specifically on the wonderful way poets use language when they write. I like to use the following poem by Mary O'Neill to highlight the way poetry explores the nuances of language. The poem is both playful and thought-provoking. In it, students can see the care O'Neill took in thinking about words, about how they sound and what they mean. Her poem invites us to do the same.

FEELINGS ABOUT WORDS

Some words clink
As ice in drink.
Some move with grace
A dance, a lace.
Some sound thin:
Wail, scream and pin.
Some words are squat:
A mug, a pot,
And some are plump,
Fat, round and dump.
Some words are light:
Drift, lift and bright.
A few are small:
A, is and all.
And some are thick,
Glue, paste and brick.
Some words are sad:
"I never had . . ."
And others gay:
Joy, spin and play.
Some words are sick:
Stab, scratch and nick.

Some words are hot:
Fire, flame and shot.
Some words are sharp,
Sword, point and carp.
And some alert:
Glint, glance and flirt.
Some words are lazy:
Saunter, hazy.
And some words preen:
Pride, pomp and queen.
Some words are quick,
A jerk, a flick.
Some words are slow:
Lag, stop and grow,
While others poke
As ox with yoke.
Some words can fly—
There's wind, there's high
And some words cry:
"Goodbye . . .
Goodbye . . . ."

In addition to the obvious rhyme—*clink* and *drink*, *preen* and *queen*—and rhythm of this poem, we are drawn into the world of words in every line. It is composed of short lines, none more than four words long, yet each one is packed full of thoughts about words. It demonstrates the capacity of words to "move with grace" or "sound thin." It is concise and full at the same time.

Choral Reading to Promote Fluency and Motivation

I share this poem with students to revel in the sound and meaning of words, and also to build fluency. After reading it to them first, I give every student a copy and use it for a choral reading, having each person read two lines in turn. We practice fluency as we feel the sound of words on our tongues. I draw attention to proper volume and enunciation by reminding them to "make sure you recite the words clearly and distinctly in a voice that all can hear." Sometimes a student will say, "Let's read it again!"—so we do. As with most fluency activities, a choral reading flows better the second time through. All of us notice a marked improvement in oral expression—an important feature of fluency—with each successive reading. I reinforce this by saying, "This poem got better each time we read it aloud." With this kind of experience, students are able to see for themselves that repeated readings of any text, long or short, improves fluency and confidence in both oral and silent reading. Through other similar experiences, repeated reading becomes a specific, useful strategy that helps them grow as independent readers. Likewise, such choral reading activities have a positive effect on motivation, making students willing and eager to do more.

Taking It Further:
Extending the Concepts of Language

I could let this poem go with only a choral reading, but because it's so jam-packed with words and concepts, it can also be used to teach word meanings and nuances. I did the following exploration with one of my classes as a natural extension of the choral reading activity.

With copies of the poem in front of us, we examined some of O'Neill's word choices. To make the experience more personal, and thereby more meaningful,

Try It Out!

WORD HUNT
AND THEN SOME

Think about how you might share this poem, using O'Neill's words to guide students on a word hunt—a search to discover similar words they know or might find in further reading. As a whole class or working in pairs, have students compose a list of words that are "plump" or "small" or "sharp." Then find other words that are "sad" or "sick" or "slow." In order to help students use reference materials in accordance with language arts standards, I like to have them use a dictionary or a thesaurus to facilitate the search. O'Neill's poem is enough to keep you going awhile. Endless possibilities. All in one poem!

Flip through poetry books to find another poem you could use with kids in such a way. Perhaps photocopy it and, on your own, circle words that are sophisticated, obscure, challenging, or vivid. Forming some of your own responses and ideas about a poem before using it with students can make you feel more sure of the genre.

I asked the class for their own examples of words that "clink, like ice in drink." They answered with "coins in a jar," "chimes in the wind," and "links on a chain." The question "Which words are 'squat'?" brought *toad*, *bowl*, and *Sumo wrestler!* Words that are "light" were *cloud*, *feather*, *heart*, *air*, and *breeze*. "Thick" words were these: *tar*, *blood*, *paint*, *cement*, and *wax*. We were on a roll! Their ideas for "sad" words ranged from "Clouds have opened" to "I am lost" and "Someone died." For words that "cry" they offered *tears*, *sigh*, and *onions!* The only problem was getting them to stop! In fact, even several days later, they were still coming up with additional words. Exploring concepts. Noticing words. Trying them out. Hearing their sounds. Sharing them with others. It becomes addictive, which is what we want to happen with language and thinking and learning.

Lesson Five: The Poet's Use of Imagery

Poetry gives us a glimpse into ourselves, others, and the world we inhabit. Whether we agree or not with a poet's perspective isn't as important as being open to that view, allowing it a place in our thoughts, and perhaps even letting it alter the way we think or feel. So often after sharing a poem, I can see the impact of the words and ideas as they settle in a student's mind or heart. I see it in a student's body language, the look on his or her face, the stillness when I finish reading. I used to think when I was met with stony silence after sharing a poem that it was a dud, or beyond students' maturity to understand. Years of sharing poetry day in and day out has proven otherwise. It is sometimes the greatest tribute to a poem that we are left speechless or with feelings inside that are difficult or too personal to express.

A poet shares his or her viewpoint in many ways: by relating an experience, advancing an opinion, or offering possibilities. But there is an especially potent device found in many poems that invites us to see things in ways we might never come to on our own. One way to achieve that vision is through imagery.

Introducing Students to Imagery

The very language of poetry enables us to imagine a different world and to see more vividly the world we already inhabit. Poetry, said Marianne Moore (in Oliver, 1994), is where we find "imaginary gardens with real toads in them." We are given "new eyes" through the poet's use of **imagery**. At the start of this lesson, I introduce the term *imagery* and provide a brief explanation of it: the poet's use of sensory details or images that appeal to our senses or that create pictures in our minds. Then I have a poem or two ready that contain vivid examples of imagery. When I share the following poem, students experience firsthand how poet Valerie Worth brings an ordinary, everyday object to life in a refreshing, dynamic way.

UMBRELLA

Slack wings
Folded, it
Hangs by a
Claw in
The closet,

Sleeping,
Or moping,
Or quietly
Hatching
A plot

To flap out
And escape
On the furious
Sweep of
The storm.

Before reading this, I say, "Think of an umbrella: its shape, its function. Listen to this poem to see if it matches what you've imagined." We bring to this poem our rather mundane notions about an umbrella—a useful yet lifeless object—and come away with our perception entirely revamped. After reading this poem, we perceive an umbrella as a living, breathing thing. In fact, it's unlikely we'll ever approach an umbrella the way we once did!

On a subsequent reading, I want to capitalize on how the poet causes this change in perception. I say, "Listen to the poem again and notice which words most clearly suggest the umbrella is alive." Students often settle on the images that come from the nouns, verbs, and modifiers in this poem, words that make vivid pictures in our minds, such as "slack wings folded," "hangs by a claw," and "quietly hatching a plot." Many of us agree that only something alive can have wings and a claw, can sleep and mope, or can hatch a plot. We envision the umbrella as a giant batlike creature—hanging, plotting, waiting to escape into the air. We fully expect the umbrella, under the right conditions, to take flight and flap away. I like to follow this up by reading other poems that make objects come alive such as selections from *Click, Rumble, Roar: Poems About Machines* (Hopkins, 1987). Poems with strong imagery help develop a deeper appreciation for poetry of all kinds and heightens our awareness of the glorious capabilities of the genre.

Through the skillful use of words in poems like "Umbrella," poets provide a fresh glimpse of the world around us. Mary Oliver (1994) says, "The language of the poem is the language of particulars. Without it, poetry might still be wise, but it would surely be pallid. And thin. It is the detailed sensory language incorporating images that gives the poem dash and tenderness. And authenticity." Poetic imagery can leave a lasting impression on our minds; words create images we not only see but also smell, taste, hear, and feel. The following selection from *Cactus Poems* by Frank Asch is appealing for this reason.

LIZARDS IN LOVE

I fell in love in the springtime,
When the air was cool and clean.
She was long and low and lovely.
Her skin was scaly and green.

I fell in love in the springtime,
When I was foolish and young.
It was love at first sight when I saw her
Catching ants on the tip of her tongue!

This poem is such a sensory favorite that every year I have individuals or entire classes who choose to memorize it. Occasional visitors to our classroom often get treated to an impromptu performance of students reciting this poem. It never fails to elicit a smile as they hear the words and "see" the images for themselves. In my experience, however, the desire to commit this poem to memory comes after we discuss its imagery. The more I can help students draw upon their senses—sight, smell, sound, touch, and taste—the more personal and effective the experience becomes and the more engaged students are in the process.

To get the most out of this poem's sensory images, I begin by reading through the poem once to get the general feel of its **theme** (love, admiration), its **tone** (friendly, conversational), and its **mood** (lighthearted, wistful). When I read it a second time, I draw attention to various parts by asking students to "imagine the feel of the desert sun on your face, and the crisp, clean air of desert springtime." In this poem, we see the image of the female lizard through the eyes of her obviously smitten male counterpart. To convey his affections authentically, students take on a dreamy, "in-love" look as we recite these words out loud together: "She was long and low and lovely. Her skin was scaly and green." By reading the words in this manner, students step into the mood or tone of the poem, which helps reinforce those literary concepts as part of the process. We close our eyes and imagine the "long, low, and lovely" look of the female lizard's body. We imagine the feel of our fingers as they touch the cool, scaly roughness of her green skin. And we especially love the vision of this enraptured male lizard when he sees the ant-catching skill of the female as she flicks her tongue in and out, in and out. Young adolescents are open and sensitive to love poems of all kinds, even between lizards, but the sensory richness of this one is its most compelling feature.

What we notice, imagine, and remember from a poem is an image of its own, an image that remains long after the initial experience of reading it. The image becomes a personal snapshot that we can keep in the scrapbook of our minds and hearts. It is the poem's legacy to us, the reader. Gregory Denman (1988) says:

> The imagery of a well-written poem begs to be preserved. It entices us to enter into the world created by the poem, to see life as the poet created it, to abandon our ordinary perceptions and experiences, and to carry with us the vision of the world as the poet sees it.

The strong images in poems such as "Umbrella" and "Lizards in Love" invite us to come into the poets' worlds, a place where we can share their creative vision. Imagery is both alluring and abundant in the genre of poetry, and it is often created through the use of figurative language. In the next lesson, I offer some ways to help students become more familiar with figurative language through simple, straightforward activities.

Lesson Six: Figurative Language

We are enticed into the world of the poet, as Denman suggests, by the particular words he or she has chosen, and the way those words are used. The language of poetry works on two levels: (1) literal, what the words actually say and mean, and (2) figurative, what the words suggest or imply. Our first entry into a poem is usually on the literal level. Frequently, however, we need to take a closer look at a poem in order to get the most out of it. Figurative devices such as **simile** and **metaphor** take us to that deeper—or higher—level. With these types of imagery, the poet uses one thing to represent another. Though more abstract than literal meaning, figurative language invites students to imagine their own vision, to ponder what they see, and to savor it. In my role as "literate mentor," I share my personal impression of the poem, directing attention to various words or phrases that inform my response, yet I remain open to student interpretation. "The words in this poem feel light and airy (or heavy and dark)," or I say, "In this poem, the poet compares his loved one to the sun. He must think she is warm and bright. What do you think?" Children often see something in a poem that I don't see. Their insight can be enlightening. And humbling! Sometimes, my view proves to be too narrow or shortsighted. The concept of "honored voice" gives each of us the right to form our own meaning and to see our own images.

Scaffolding Students' Understanding of Figurative Language

Although figurative meaning is not as immediately apparent or accessible as literal meaning, understanding it is not beyond the grasp of even younger children. Students of any age, however, including those in the middle school, benefit from some direct instruction to ease them into it. Considering Vygotsky's (1986) "zone of proximal development"—the area between what a child can do on her own and what she can do with assistance—I take on the role of "more knowledgeable other" with my students. I scaffold their understanding of figurative language—or any poetic element—in simple ways. With a little initial help, students are soon able to grasp more sophisticated examples on their own.

Understanding how figurative language works and how it differs from literal meaning can be confusing. To help sort that out early in the school year, I provide direct instruction on how to think in figurative ways. I've found it works well to start with the identity students know best—the self— in helping students grasp the way poets use figurative language. I often begin by asking them to respond through discussion or in their writing journals to questions such as: "How are you like a flower? A rock? An old shoe?" Together we explore the qualities and characteristics of an item or object and then compare it to ourselves. Using myself as a model for this activity, I offer something like: "I am like a flower when I am growing, unfolding, and becoming more of who I am." Next, students write or share their own ideas on how they compare to a flower, or a rock, or an old shoe. From there, students need only travel a short distance to make comparisons involving other people and things. I help them explore this kind of thinking by asking questions such as: "How is your mother like a blanket?" Or I have them fill in the blank: "My best friend is like a _____." In a group discussion, we compare two unlike things by finding a common trait: "How is the moon like a mirror? A thought like a butterfly?" It often helps to list students' responses on chart paper labeled FIGURATIVE LANGUAGE and post it somewhere in the room for future reference. This keeps the concept of figurative language available for review.

Next, I continue instruction in figurative language by naming and defining the literary devices of simile and metaphor and sharing poetry that contains one or both. My explanation of these terms is simple and focuses on the distinction between them: a simile uses *like* or *as* in its comparison (e.g., "Juliet is *like* the sun"), while a metaphor makes a direct comparison ("Juliet *is* the sun"). Since the following poem by Pablo Neruda uses both of these devices, I use it to help students see the distinctions.

ODE TO ENCHANTED LIGHT

Under the trees light
has dropped from the top of the sky,
light
like a green
latticework of branches,
shining
on every leaf,
drifting down like clean
white sand.

A cicada sends
its sawing song
high into the empty air.

The world is
a glass overflowing
with water.

Working together as a group, we identify the similes in the poem: "light *like* a green lattice-work of branches," "drifting down *like* clean white sand," and then the metaphors: "light has dropped," "a cicada sends its sawing song," "the world *is* a glass overflowing with water." These specific examples from the poem help reinforce the concepts I've taught through direct instruction, and can now be added to the chart under the labels SIMILE and METAPHOR.

Poetry with Strong Imagery

"Caged Bird" by Maya Angelou

"There Is No Frigate Like a Book"
by Emily Dickinson

"Hold Fast Your Dreams" by Louise Driscoll

"The Road Not Taken" by Robert Frost

"Blackberry Eating" by Galway Kinnell

"Catalogue" by Rosalie Moore

"Pet Rock" by Cynthia Rylant

"Fog" by Carl Sandburg

"Lobster" by Anne Sexton

"Sonnet 18" by William Shakespeare

BOOKS:

Touch the Poem by Arnold Adoff

Echoes for the Eye: Poems to Celebrate Patterns in Nature by Barbara Juster Esbensen

The Dream Keeper and Other Poems by Langston Hughes

The Place My Words Are Looking For selected by Paul B. Janeczko

This Big Sky by Pat Mora

Come With Me: Poems for a Journey by Naomi Shihab Nye

The Leaf and the Cloud by Mary Oliver

Hailstones and Halibut Bones by Mary O'Neill

A Child's Anthology of Poetry edited by Elizabeth Hauge Sword

Night Garden: Poems from the World of Dreams by Janet S. Wong

By now, I've given students a demonstration lesson of figurative language (with me as the "subject" under discussion), asked them to write and/or discuss comparisons between themselves and another object, defined important literary terms, shared a poem rich in figurative language and identified both simile and metaphor in it, and created a class-generated reference chart that will review and reinforce the concepts we've explored. All the facets of this lesson enable students to take the next step in exploring figurative language—writing their own examples of similes and metaphors. Examples of student exploration of figurative language can be found in Chapter 5 (family/friend poems) and Chapter 6 (metaphors in response to "Mother to Son").

In the type of lesson described here, students experience the way poets create comparisons and begin to appreciate how images come alive through the use of vivid description. As you adapt my ideas to your own style or needs and see how readily students respond, you will be encouraged to continue sharing poetry that is particularly rich in imagery and figurative language. Happily for everyone, such poetry can be found easily and in abundance. See the box at left for some of my favorites.

TRUSTING THE VOICE OF POETRY

This chapter presented foundation lessons that explore the unique characteristics of poetry and provide definitions of key terms so you and your students can engage in discussions about poems and their common elements with more ease and confidence. If the genre is relatively new to you or uncharted territory in your instruction, you may have to overcome the notion that you can't teach something well unless you've had plenty of experience. Learning to navigate through poetry should be a joyful journey. Read poetry each day to become familiar with rhythm, rhyme scheme, stanzas, style, and theme. As you discuss these common features with your class on a regular basis, everyone—both you and them—will become more comfortable working with the genre.

Let there be plenty of poetry experiences, however, in which the poem is simply read and heard and savored. Poet William Stafford (1978) says that analyzing poetry too much is like "boiling a watch to find out what makes it tick." The following work by Billy Collins gives some great advice about how to treat a poem—and how not to treat a poem.

INTRODUCTION TO POETRY

I ask them to take a poem
and hold it up to the light
like a color slide

or press an ear against its hive.

I say drop a mouse into a poem
and watch him probe his way out,

or walk inside the poem's room
and feel the walls for a light switch.

I want them to waterski
across the surface of a poem
waving at the author's name on the shore.

But all they want to do
is tie the poem to a chair with rope
and torture a confession out of it.

They begin beating it with a hose
to find out what it really means.

Collins, as a teacher and a poet, offers an important message. He suggests we simply enter a poem with our hearts in the right place—there is no need to tear the poem apart or poke it with a sharp stick till it gives up its meaning. Instead of being frightened by this freedom, I hope you will feel comforted and encouraged. Trust what he says. Trust poetry to speak its own voice. And trust your students to hear it.

The next chapter takes up the cause of bringing poetry to the classroom, putting it in the hands of students, and providing opportunities for them to respond to the voice they hear in a poem either through reflective writing or group discussion.

CHAPTER THREE

Thinking, Talking, and Writing About Poetry:
Generating Enthusiastic, Thoughtful Responses

A poem is not a ready-made object to which a reader is passively exposed. A poem is a happening, an event, in which the listener or reader draws on images and feelings and ideas stirred up by the words of the text; out of these is shaped the lived-through experience.

~ Louise M. Rosenblatt

In the previous chapter, I discussed the basics of poetry with lessons and suggested poems to use in the early weeks of school to help you and your students achieve a comfort level and familiarity with the genre and to establish a common vocabulary to make discussion easier. This chapter continues the conversation about sharing poetry on a regular basis and, in the process, getting students to think, talk, and write about poetry.

If you want to use poetry to create a classroom that promotes the joy of reading and language, fosters the role of the reader, and advances language arts standards across the curriculum, then reader response theory—specifically Rosenblatt's Transactional Theory—is a critical component of a philosophy that will guide you toward those goals. What are the features that distinguish this view of the reading process? What dynamics are at work? And how does reader response theory support the use of poetry and inform our practices with poetry in the classroom? A brief look at the development and principles of reader response theory might help.

READER RESPONSE THEORY

Many years ago—before the academic world knew much about reader response theory—Louise Rosenblatt was busy observing and reflecting on the process by which students engaged with literature. Her views—especially those that emphasized the importance of the literary experience as a framework for a philosophy of teaching—were considered by many to have been both powerfully influential and ahead of their time. Rosenblatt was greatly influenced by her own experience as a teacher as well as a student, and over a period of many years her Transactional Theory of reading emerged. This theory stood in sharp contrast to the philosophy of New Criticism, which held that meaning is embedded in the text and it is the reader's job to find it. New Critics proposed the "affective fallacy"—the idea that any consideration of the reader's emotions as contributing to meaning was misguided. And then along came Rosenblatt to turn that kind of thinking on its ear.

Rosenblatt's work was among the first to seriously recognize and advance the importance of the reader. In 1938, Rosenblatt wrote *Literature as Exploration*, a major pedagogical study that describes a reciprocal relationship between text and the reader. One is not privileged over the other, she says; rather, there is a back-and-forth interplay between the two. There is no such thing, in Rosenblatt's view, as a generic reader or a generic text. The reading act occurs with a particular reader with a particular text at a particular time. Thus, there can be as many potential "meanings" as there are individual reading acts or, said another way, as many personal responses as there are readers.

Reading as Transaction: Efferent and Aesthetic Stance

In her later work, *The Reader, the Text, the Poem: The Transactional Theory of the Literary Work* (1978), Rosenblatt provides a theoretical model for the relationship between reader and text. Her transactional theory proposes the existence of two kinds of transactions, efferent and aesthetic, which designate the reader's predominant stance, or purpose, during the reading act. These two stances can be thought of as opposite ends of a continuum along which a reader can move freely, back and forth, during any reading act, depending on one's purpose or mindset.

In her writing and ongoing work, Rosenblatt raises concerns over the dominance in mainstream education of efferent reading (from the Latin, *effere*, "to carry away"), which asks students to read for facts and information; to analyze, reason, and synthesize; a stance that focuses on what is to be taken away and retained after the reading event. Stance is most often determined by the types of questions teachers ask before the reading. If I ask my students, for example, to read a poem to discover the theme or rhyme scheme or to locate facts, I'm expecting them to adopt an efferent stance to elicit a cognitive response.

Rosenblatt believes, however, that reading involves not only the mind but also the emotions of a reader, and that emphasis on efferent reading occurs at the expense of aesthetic reading (from the Greek word meaning "to sense" or "to perceive"), which focuses instead on the images, feelings, and sensations that come up during the reading act. Far too often, in her view, teachers with a "testing motive" steer students toward an efferent response, often resulting in routine or shallow reading, rather than adopting an aesthetic stance that would lead to a deeper, more personal, or affective, response. Asking students "What does this poem remind you of?" or "What feelings or images come up when you read this?" gives attention to aesthetic response. According to Rosenblatt (1980), it is this often neglected yet highly important aesthetic stance that helps the reader shape meaning from her "lived-through experience—her thoughts, emotions, images, and so forth, that become part of the overall reading event and help her create meaning from the text." In the realm of literature, there is hardly a more immediate way to achieve a "lived-through experience" than through the reading of a poem.

POETRY: A LIVED-THROUGH EXPERIENCE

Poetry's effect on Emily Dickinson was dramatic, the lived-through experience obvious. Her reaction to reading poetry—that she felt "physically as if the top of [her] head were taken off"—is a perfect illustration of the evocative power of poetry or other literature to resonate uniquely within each of us. It is this highly personal response that Rosenblatt believes is so important during and after a reading event. In the teaching of literature, she encourages selective attention to the "inner states, the kinesthetic tensions, the colorings of the stream of consciousness that accompany all cognition." Thus, feelings, emotions, images, memories, impressions, past experiences, and spontaneous reactions are all essential components of aesthetic response to poetry. By forging such personal connections first, we increase the likelihood that students will care about a poem's broader meaning during subsequent readings and discussion. In a practical sense, aesthetic response can serve as a gateway to other layers of meaning or responses to a poem. Teachers are the vital link in creating the kind of classroom environment where such responses are welcomed and celebrated.

How do we create such a place? The next section offers some ideas to consider.

Creating a Safe Environment for Student Response

There are many dynamics involved in creating a safe, inviting classroom where students and poetry can flourish. It takes time, care, and attention to establish this kind of receptive atmosphere. As teachers, we must make mindful choices along the way, choices that compel us to examine our various roles, consider the individual needs and personalities of our students, and demonstrate respect for both student and poetry as we bring the two together. Let me share some thoughts about each of these concerns.

The Teacher as Literate Mentor

Students are impressionable creatures, vulnerable to the style and personality of each teacher. They look to us, as well as at us, for cues about attitude, behavior, expectations, and process. We are powerful role models in many ways, and perhaps none is more important than the role of "literate mentor." From this position, we act in ways that become almost automatic: we model fluent reading,

10 Key Concepts of Reader Response Theory

❋ Both the reader and the text are important in the reading process.

❋ Reading is a transaction between a reader and a text at a particular time under particular circumstances.

❋ Stance refers to the reader's purpose or mindset during or after the reading event.

❋ Every reading act falls somewhere on a continuum between predominantly efferent and predominantly aesthetic reading.

❋ The reader needs to adopt a predominant stance—efferent or aesthetic—to guide the reading process; any text can be read either way.

❋ The reader's stance during the reading event directly affects what emerges from the reading.

❋ Efferent stance focuses attention on what is to be retained, recalled, analyzed, paraphrased, etc., *after* the reading event.

❋ Aesthetic stance focuses primarily on what is being personally lived through, cognitively and affectively, *during* the reading event.

❋ The reader's selective attention during aesthetic reading focuses on what is evoked through the words of a text and then brought to one's consciousness.

❋ The impressions, images, reactions, and emotions that are evoked constitute the "lived-through experience."

we "think aloud" as we read text to demonstrate what good readers do, we suggest particular strategies in response to specific needs, we familiarize students with different genres and authors, we attempt to put the right books into each reader's hands. But this is just a start.

Our role as literate mentor is much more than what we do; it includes the attitudes we bring into our classroom and into our relationship with students. I care very much, for example, that my students grow to love the act of reading, to love books, and to love the ideas and people and places we meet in those books. I convey this message in many ways. The very way I touch a book, turn it over in my hands, gaze at the cover illustration, wonder aloud about its contents, or share brief impressions of the poet's or author's work speaks volumes about the respect and even reverence I have for the written word. This poem by Emily Dickinson captures the essence of my actions and beliefs.

A WORD IS DEAD

A word is dead
When it is said,
Some say.
I say it just
Begins to live
That day.

This poem reminds me that as much as I love books, my highest regard should be for the beings in front of me, the students who are waiting and watching and listening to what I say. I honor the work by sharing it, but I honor my students by offering it to them. So when I bring a poem or a book of poetry before them, I am in essence saying, "These words form a remarkable thing—a poem—and you, remarkable beings yourselves, are worthy of this work. I trust you to receive it, to treat it with care and consideration." And then I show them how to do that. I start by valuing what they think and feel.

Repeat After Me: "No One Right Meaning!"

In creating a safe environment for personal response, we may need to undo a few old behaviors or misconceptions along the way. Earlier in this book, I wrote that many teachers and older students dislike poetry as a result of negative classroom experiences with it. The biggest complaint mentioned from those earlier school memories centers around how to derive meaning from a poem or, more to the point, who gets to decide the meaning. Students of all ages (and remember, we were all students once!) resent being told there is one sacred meaning for a poem, usually that of the teacher or the absent poet, who is in no position to help when it comes time to "decode" the elusive meaning, nebulous theme, or obscure references in his or her poem. And I could be wrong here, but I'm fairly certain that the poets themselves, if they were privy to these classroom ordeals, would resent this practice even more than we did! What poet could be gratified by the picking apart of the poem, piece by painful piece, until there is nothing left of it but a scrawny carcass? Not a pretty sight.

Luckily, most of us don't go quite that far in our search to extract meaning from a poem. Meaning sometimes emerges easily and naturally. But now and then a poem defies understanding and often asks more questions than it answers. Liz Rosenberg (1998) writes of this elusive quality of poetry:

> I would say that it is all right to be partly confused by a poem; it's all right if you can only grab hold of one corner of it, because eventually that corner may be enough to pull you all the way through. Sometimes we love poetry because we don't completely understand it.

Our role is to help students grab a corner or two of a given poem, to be open to what the poem reveals to each of us, and then to allow each student to hold on to that personal revelation—whatever it is.

Right now, this very minute, repeat these words like a mantra (and say them out loud if that helps you remember!): "There is no one right meaning to a poem. There is no one right meaning to a poem. There is no one right meaning to a poem." Embracing this position frees you up to be a facilitator, not the arbiter, of a poem's meaning. There is much less pressure, and certainly more pleasure, when you take this stance. Don't you feel better already?!

Respecting the Individual

If there is no one right meaning, then what Louise Rosenblatt said is true: there are as many possible meanings to a poem as there are individual readers. Though we use the text of a poem as a guide or a compass, the road to personal meaning sometimes takes unpredictable twists and turns or even detours. So how do we help students arrive there? How do we make room for personal response that is diverse or unconventional?

Just for a minute, ponder what it means to be an individual. We are many different things—teacher, student, friend, spouse, sibling, child, parent, grandparent, lover, advocate, aunt/uncle, colleague, writer, reader, gardener, traveler, and on and on. Add several of your own labels to the list. Every one of them is on board with us when we read a poem. We react in different ways, depending on which facets of ourselves are most affected or interested or involved. The same is true of students, who are, after all, just younger versions of ourselves. If we have a right to be uniquely ourselves, with our own experiences and idiosyncrasies, we must allow for such individual differences in our students as well. In other words, personal response is and should be . . . personal! Nancie Atwell (1987) writes: "Poetry requires personal response more so than any other genre, because a poem is such an intensely personal response to the world." When we do what is necessary to create a safe atmosphere in our classroom, intensely personal responses to poetry can emerge and be heard. The road to meaning is a journey shared by many travelers, each with his or her own voice. Each voice adds something worthwhile to the trip.

The Concept of "Honored Voice"

Honoring student voice is the bedrock for building a safe classroom environment, one that values and respects individual student response to poetry. In one study, Penny Oldfather (in Perfect, 1997) discovered a classroom that emphasized and promoted student construction of meaning as well as a "deep responsiveness" to student expression, a concept she calls "honored voice." Students in that classroom said that the qualities they considered most important in a teacher were that he or she be caring, understanding, trusting, and respectful of students' ideas, opinions, and feelings. These are the traits we strive for, the ones we will nurture in ourselves to help students feel safe, valued, and vital to the literate community of our classroom. By accepting without judgment (though not

How to Create a Safe Environment for Personal Response

Adopt a "no one right meaning" position.

- A poem is open to individual interpretation and meaning.
- Be the facilitator, not the arbiter, of a poem's meaning.

Promote the concept of "honored voice."

- Each voice matters and has a right to be heard.
- Diverse ideas are an integral part of a healthy, vibrant literate community.

Use comments that demonstrate student response is worthy and welcome.

- "That's an interesting idea."
- "You give us something to think about; I appreciate your thoughts."
- "Does anyone have a different view?"

Establish classroom procedures that promote respect and unity.

- Involve students in deciding procedural guidelines.
- Encourage student collaboration activities.
- Treat differing views courteously and without criticism.

Support exploration of personal response through modeling and guidance.

- Share connections made between poems and your own life.
- Use "think-alouds" to guide students through various levels of response.

Allow for personal choice regarding poetry and student response to it.

- Provide a variety of response opportunities (oral, written, artistic, and so on).

always without guidance) what students contribute, we communicate to them that we honor each voice, that we believe each one adds to the symphony of classroom response. Individual personal response has a place to thrive in such an environment. Where voices thrive, so can poetry.

Forms of Response: Internal and External

Personal response to poetry is more likely when individuals have a safe place to have their own voice. But creating a safe environment is just the first step in the process of developing deep and meaningful response to poems of all types. Meaningful response to poetry falls within two major categories: (1) a more private, internal response and (2) a more public, external one. They are complementary, with one informing and enhancing the other. Each is an integral part of the overall pattern of reader response in the classroom.

At first, I need to show students the possibilities when responding to poetry, and that it's okay to have an internal, personal, and private response to a poem. After all, this is where response begins—on the inside—and many times a poem evokes such strong feelings that an individual needs to hold that in for a while, to process the emotions and ideas that arise, and to follow them along to see where they lead. It may be that a poem elicits a personal connection to one's life, or speaks directly to the heart or soul in some way; certain poetry is distinctive for its sound or look, or the way it causes us to visualize images as we read it. These initial internal impressions, thoughts, and feelings can become external forms of response. Once students are comfortable responding internally and paying attention to what comes up, I encourage them to bring that forward into the open and share it in more public, external ways.

The way these two forms of response develop in my own classroom takes time and follows a predictable path. In the beginning of a school year, many students are tentative about offering their internal responses: their thoughts, impressions, emotions, and such. They seem to need a fair amount of modeling on my part, usually in the form of "think alouds" or what I would characterize as spontaneous reactions or musings regarding a poem's words, theme, or images.

- This poem always makes me feel a little melancholy since it makes me think of my father who died.

- When I read this poem, I feel like I should whisper because its theme is so somber and "heavy."

- Here's a poem about love that makes me smile inside and out. What images did the poet use to help us visualize his loved one?

- I wonder why the poet repeated certain words so many times?

- Since I'm a parent, this poem about a deaf child makes me grateful and sad all at once.

- How do you think the poet writing this poem must have felt? Angry? Afraid?

- I like how this poem surprises us at the end… like a punch!

I make these kinds of comments before, during, or after reading a poem to help students get comfortable navigating their own way through poetry. This modeling is an essential and natural type of scaffold technique, especially if students are unfamiliar with poetry as a genre, or haven't had much experience with poetry of different styles. My think-alouds help show students *how* to think, not *what* to think, as they formulate personal responses to poetry. I'm the journeyman, so to speak, and they, as my apprentices, have much to learn. As literate mentor—or "more knowledge-able other"—I model ways of responding to poetry that are simple and personal without being condescending or didactic.

Take, for example, the poem "Mother's Biscuits" by Freda Quenneville. Before reading it aloud, I share some brief anecdotal comments about spending many hours in my mother's kitchen while growing up, and how this poem reminds me of the sights, sounds, aromas, and tastes that came from that kitchen. Then I say, "As you listen, think of the images or memories stirred up for you." Next I read the poem, taking my time with the lines, to let the images form in our minds and stimulate the senses.

MOTHER'S BISCUITS

In a big bowl she'd fluff in flour,
Make a fist-dent
For buttermilk and lard which she squeezed
Between her fingers
The way a child goes at a mud puddle,
Raking dry flour
From the sides until it mixed right.

She'd give the dough a pat for luck,
Nip a springy bud,
Roll it round and flat-it-down
With a motion
Continued to a grease-shined pan.
Mother's biscuits
Cooked high, crusty, with succulent middles
That took attention
At company dinners; but on kitchen-nights
They were finest
Soaked with pot liquor or gravy.

And those rich biscuits could put a shine
On Sunday patent
That let the Lord know who was there.
A panful stood
Ready as magic at dawn's light:
I'd take some
When leaving late to the schoolbus
And up the road
I'd run, puffing through biscuit crumbs
My haloed breath
Into the skin-sharp morning air.

I end by telling them of my mother's baking, especially her pies with their flaky crusts, creamy filling, and delicate meringue, and how on pie-baking day she would make me a miniature crust with sugar and cinnamon so I'd have my own child-size pie to eat. Many poems can be found to call upon such memories of personal experience.

I often expect silence to follow the reading of poems like "Mother's Biscuits," allowing time for private recall of students' own memories of sights, smells, tastes, sounds, and touch. In the beginning weeks of a school year, I don't push too hard or expect too much in the form of student response. I trust that there is something going on internally even if there is no obvious or outward verbal response, on their part. By making my own "inner voice" public through the modeling process and asking students to simply consider, ponder, and reflect privately, I'm setting the stage for more public forms of response, such as reflective writing and class discussion, two common types of response to poetry.

SHARING PERSONAL RESPONSE THROUGH REFLECTIVE WRITING

Once students see from teacher modeling that response can be simple and straightforward, and a few of them begin to risk making their internal thoughts public through their own verbal reactions, personal response begins to find its way into the ethos of the classroom. Each class is different, of course, but generally speaking it takes only a few weeks for student response to poetry to become external. On my part, I make sure to be accepting and respectful of what students offer as they share thoughts openly: "I can see your point; I appreciate your sharing that." During this early phase of more public, open sharing of personal response, I gently encourage others to share their views by asking, "Does anyone have other ideas (reactions, feelings, etc.) about this poem, or something that confuses, bothers, or excites you in it?" Such questions are designed to be open-ended and to invite other voices into the mix.

Some students, however, enjoy the relative safety of writing their personal responses rather than sharing aloud, at least at first. With this in mind, I like to provide occasional opportunities for reflective writing in poetry response journals, or on notebook paper, as a way to tap into what and how students think of individual poems. Here's a list of typical questions I might ask to prompt their thinking and writing:

- What images do you notice or wonder about in this poem?

- What memories or reactions come up for you as you read/listen to this poem?

- What does this poem make you think about?

- What feelings are you aware of as you read/listen to the poem?

- What works especially well for you in this poem (e.g., topic, word choice, rhyme scheme, etc.)?

- Is there anything disturbing or confusing about this poem?

- What would you like to tell or ask the poet regarding this poem?

Depending on the particular poem, I usually select two or three of these prompts, jot them on the board, and ask students to write about them. This is by no means an exhaustive list of possibilities, but some I've found useful in getting a good variety of personal responses from students. The grade level of students, of course, will help determine which questions you ask and what to expect in terms of how complex or sophisticated their responses will be.

To keep interest vibrant, it's a good idea to balance reflective writing with other forms of written response by varying what you ask students to write. One time it might be a journal entry or reader response log in which they write a paragraph or several short ones based on questions like those listed above. Most often, this written response is done in class for 10 to 15 minutes or so, but it can also be an "at-home" assignment. Other times, you might say, "In one minute or less, write down as many impressions of this poem as you can. Responses should be short phrases or single words that come to mind as you read or listen to the poem." With this type of stream-of-consciousness writing activity, internal personal response becomes external, you get a sense of what students think or feel, and you're getting this information over a relatively short period of time. If one minute is too short, give them three or five. Choose what feels appropriate for your students' age and ability and the particular poem's interest level and content.

Sometimes my students use a simple response form with three open-ended statements (*The poem made me feel...*, *Images I thought of...*, and *Words I liked...*) to write their impressions of a poem, such as the following one by Tony Johnston:

COWS

Where the old barn　　　　　　*then slow as summer*
slumps in the sun,　　　　　　*wander*
they browse for clumps　　　　*down to the fence*
of poppies　　　　　　　　　　*and stretch to reach*
between the spokes of a broken　*lavender lupine.*
wheel,

Here are a few thoughts students wrote on the response form.

The poem made me feel:

relaxed and soothed

drowsy

like eating and going to pick flowers

tired, like I should take a nap

like I wanted to just lie down and watch the cows eat

Images I thought of:

cows reaching out their necks and eating

an old barn and poppies swaying in the wind

green grass, brown cows, shining sun, walking down a fence line

bees buzzing and cows wandering in a pasture

slow ice cream dripping in a cup and many cows coming to me

Words I liked:

slumps in the sun

browse

slumps and clumps

wander

lavender lupine

Before handing in their completed forms, students selected one idea from each of the three open-ended sections and shared it with the class, as in the following example: "The poem made me feel peaceful and relaxed, I saw an image of an old red barn, and I liked the word *browse*." Creating a simple response form such as this one provides a quick and easy way for students to respond to various poems. Mix it up with other formats and other writing prompts, then use their written impressions and ideas to spark further response through conversation about individual poems.

Quick and Easy Written Responses

1. Respond to a prompt.
2. Quick writes.
3. Open-ended responses.

SHARING PERSONAL RESPONSE THROUGH DISCUSSION

While writing is an important method of eliciting student response, personal response to poetry takes place most often through discussion. After students are immersed for a few weeks in daily poetry sharing, conversations about poetry begin to happen naturally. Teacher modeling is critical, however, as you guide them into becoming involved along with you in discussions. Briefly, here's how it usually evolves.

Initially, a handful of students may make a comment or two in response to a poem I've read. Once others learn that responses are accepted without criticism and given respectful guidance, more students become involved in the dialogue. At first, you'll want to keep discussions relatively short and lively. Gradually, you'll develop awareness of when to extend the conversation, how to direct it, and where the poem itself is calling you to go. With daily or frequent poetry experience, students take up discussion as a normal occurrence. Share a poem, respond to poem. Share a poem, respond to poem. Breathe in, breathe out.

As with other genres and curriculum areas, poetry conversations generally occur in two main types of discussion formats: whole-class and peer-led. In the following sections, I'll describe each one and give suggestions for putting them into practice. I'll also include some ideas about eliciting response from students, and offer a few thoughts on how to handle occasional obstacles or resistance. For an example of a class discussion, see pages 112–115.

Leading Whole-Class Discussion

In my experience, whole-group discussion is by far the more common format for talking about poetry. Regularly planned class discussions enable students to take up a poem in an increasingly natural way, resulting in satisfying conversations in response to it. Setting up class discussion with your own students need not be difficult. Here are some steps that may help you.

When class time is at a premium, whole-group discussions can take place with students seated wherever their desks are positioned in the room, in clusters or rows, but I prefer moving them into a circle or horseshoe-shaped grouping so everyone can see each other as we converse. There's something equalizing about a circle, with no one behind or hidden in back of someone else. I also find it's easier to hear one another when we're face to face this way. Once we're settled and positioned in a comfortable way, sharing and discussing a poem can begin. I try to plan a whole-class discussion roughly once a week, with discussion lasting at least 20 minutes, but if the response is lively and engaging, it's not unusual to spend an entire class period (about 45 minutes) on one poem.

For a planned poetry discussion, I start by telling students I have a poem to share and that we'll discuss it after I read it. I usually mention the poem's topic, theme, or style, and some brief anecdotal information about the poet if it's something I know to be accurate: "Here's a poem about a lost love: 'Annabel Lee,' written by Edgar Allan Poe, a poet known for his melancholy and the dark or heavy mood conveyed in his work." Or another example: "Poet Ogden Nash (who would name their newborn baby boy Ogden?!) wrote wildly clever and humorous poetry using well-crafted meter and rhyme schemes. This one, 'Adventures of Isabel,' tells about a gutsy little girl who meets all challenges head-on." Following this brief introduction, I read the poem through once. After this initial reading, I may draw attention to a particular feature found in the poem such as repetition or imagery. Then I read the poem again a second time. Our discussion takes off from there.

Let me offer a word or two here about how to equip students for discussions about poetry. With planned poetry shares and discussions, the ones I want to guide into longer, more involved conversations, it is usually a good idea for students to see as well as hear the poem we're going to discuss. I can't reasonably expect students to remember or memorize important aspects of a poem just from hearing me read it once or even twice. With this in mind, I give each student his own copy of the poem to refer to as we discuss it. This way, students can comment on specific features of the poem they might not otherwise notice from merely listening to it (e.g., line breaks). They have their own printed copy to reread and use in writing notes, highlighting certain words or phrases, and/or making other notational marks and comments. In the case of my regular, daily poetry share, however, it's neither practical nor necessary to distribute copies of every poem I choose, so most of the time students simply listen as I read the poem. Then we either engage in a brief discussion of it or let the pleasure of the experience stand on its own merits.

Starting the Conversation... and Keeping It Going

To get the conversational ball rolling, I sometimes offer a quick personal comment in response to the poem ("Now, that poem really disturbed me!") or I throw out an open-ended question similar to the ones mentioned earlier in the chapter as writing prompts: "What did you notice or wonder as you heard/read this poem?" The beauty of these types of questions is how wide open they are. One student might notice line length or rhyme scheme; another might notice the serious mood of the poem; still others may mention line breaks.

Remember, however, that this is about personal response to poetry and what a particular poem evokes in the reader, so if discussion gets stuck on the "mechanics" of poetry and doesn't appear to be moving past that, I ask a more direct question, such as "What feelings or reactions did you have upon hearing this poem?" or "What did this make you think of in your own life?" This kind of question often helps reroute the dialogue toward more personal connections and responses. Also, I remind myself that even though I want to facilitate and not manage our discussion, I sometimes have to model ways of thinking and sharing personal response to poetry in order to sustain or move the discussion along. This is especially true as I introduce students to increasingly complex or sophisticated poetry, or a type of poetry they've not yet encountered. Each new experience will require some simple scaffolding. I am not shy about providing it with well-placed think-alouds to give them the modeling they need. My voice is part of the mix, and I have the right to an opinion or personal response, too!

Sometimes, maybe even most of the time, you will share a poem simply for enjoyment and with no expectation or plan that it will end in discussion. When students have been involved on a regular basis with planned poetry discussions, spontaneous conversations begin to occur as a matter of course. When this happens (and I can almost guarantee it will!), let the conversation flow, however short-lived or sustained it becomes. Trust your instincts about how to direct or facilitate the discussion, using the same guidelines offered above or in previous chapters. Consider this an encouraging sign that poetry has taken root in the hearts and minds of your students.

One year, I asked students to complete an opinion survey regarding discussion formats (whole-class vs. peer-led). Here is what some of them wrote about whole-class discussion:

I prefer whole-group discussion because when people talk, it makes me think of some things I might not have thought of.

Not everybody participates.

In whole-group discussion, there aren't as many mishaps because the teacher is there.

Whole-group works best when Mrs. Perfect suggests something and it sparks an idea.

I get nervous and hate to talk in front of everyone.

I like to hear what everyone has to say.

I like it more with Mrs. Perfect there; everyone listens better.

Wait Time

There are plenty of times I've just about given up a poem for dead, ready to relegate it to the "failed poetry" pile, when a student's hand pops up in the classroom somewhere—and the conversation is off and running. All it takes is some patience on my part, and a willingness to let silence surround us for a bit, before throwing in the proverbial poetry towel. *Give time time*, the saying goes. It's wise to remember this when you reach those awkward moments that seem to be going nowhere.

I don't like that we get off the subject sometimes.

I like the way we get sidetracked.

Did you notice the interesting dichotomy of student opinions? Some students enjoy the richness of whole-class talk; some hate talking in front of a large group. Some students like getting sidetracked; others don't! Not every poem will speak to every student, of course. But for those students who always seem to shrink into the background of whole-class discussion or get real small in their seats to make themselves invisible, I think their response is less about poetry than about their fear of speaking in front of others. I handle these students as gently as possible. I have to be a careful observer as I search their faces for the possibility of a response that's just beneath the surface, waiting and wanting to come out. I try not to put them on the spot or make them uncomfortable, but I do try to encourage quiet students by saying something like: "Sue, it looks like you're having a thought about what's being discussed. Can you tell us what you think? Do you agree or disagree?" This last question—"Do you agree or disagree?"—is easy to answer with one word or the other, but almost always a student will elaborate, even if only briefly, which helps them feel a part of the class discussion.

We can't please everyone in every instance, so I accept that there will be individual preferences in poetry as well as in how to respond to it. In light of these differences, my job is to provide a variety of ways for students to react to poetry—through writing, conversation, or other creative activities—so that students have the chance to respond, at least some of the time, in the way they prefer. Peer-led discussion groups, which I take up in the next section, are one of those possibilities.

Guiding Peer-Led Discussion

Once whole-class discussions of poetry have become established and students have gotten comfortable sharing their responses in that format, I like to introduce yet another way of having poetry conversations—through peer-led discussion groups. How often you plan for this, like most things, is an individual choice, but I like to have them twice a month or so. Some classes really take to this format, and if that's the case, I increase their frequency to once a week.

The basic setup for peer-led discussion is fairly simple. Students are divided into groups of four to six people, desks or chairs are arranged in a circle, and everyone has a copy of the poem to consult during discussion. (Whenever possible, I move a couple of groups into the hallway just outside the room to minimize distractions from nearby voices.) Before having our first discussion in this format, we spend part or most of one class period discussing characteristics of peer-led discussion and positive group dynamics—everyone participates, no one should dominate or interrupt others, we listen respectfully to other views, and so on. During this discussion, I also add that one way to keep discussion focused is by referring often to the text of the poem when sharing personal responses.

Each group designates a student facilitator to mediate the discussion. In advance of starting peer-led conversations, we discuss the responsibilities of the student facilitator, which are: (1) to participate in discussion as a regular group member and (2) to move discussion along in various ways. We talk about specific ways a peer facilitator can help discussions succeed. For example, she can:

- direct questions to the more hesitant members of the group: "What do you think about this, Andy?"

- draw out longer responses: "Would you explain that idea a little more?"

- keep the discussion on track: "Let's talk about the imagery or unusual words in this poem."

These are the same kinds of guiding statements or questions I typically use during whole-class discussions. Student facilitators are also responsible for trying to keep the conversation balanced so no single member dominates the group: "Carla, why don't we let others respond to what you've shared." Each time we have a peer-led discussion, we appoint a new student facilitator so everyone has a turn at it. Some students are naturals at keeping things going with their peers while others find it more problematic. They all seem to appreciate my job a little bit more in the process!

Starting the Discussion

Once roles and procedures are clear, I usually start the discussion process by reading the poem I've selected to the whole group. I ask them to reread the poem within their groups, either aloud or to themselves, before discussion begins. Then, to get the conversation going, I may offer a leading question, such as, "What feelings or memories come up for you as you read/listen to this poem? Be ready to talk about them with your group." To add and to give more autonomy to the groups, it's good to have one of the members bring a poem to the session; this would be assigned a few days in advance to give the students enough time to find it and to check it with me before the actual discussion session occurs. They either choose from my poetry books or ones they find on their own.

The first few times we do peer-led groups, it helps to have a list of prompts written on the board or overhead, or printed on the same sheet as the copy of the poem. (Refer to the questions on page 55 for examples.) Before long, students will begin to use these prompts automatically to help carry the conversation and won't need to see them written out each time. These prompts guide the students into exploring different aspects of response, often resulting in a more comprehensive discussion. And then I fade into the shadows, in a sense, and let the peers discuss!

During an actual peer-led discussion, I act as a "roving facilitator" as I circulate through the room, staying in the background of student discussions. I spend only a few minutes at a time with individual groups, and if I say anything at all, it is usually in the form of a quick question or comment to redirect or kick-start a stalled discussion before moving on.

Just as whole-class discussion will sometimes be short-lived or last an entire class period, there is no set time limit for discussing poetry in peer-led groups. I select poems I think will offer rich possibilities, but that doesn't always work out. What clicks with me may fall flat with students. I would say a discussion session should last no less than 15 to 20 minutes and more likely will be closer to 30 minutes or even more, depending on the success of the poem. This includes time to get set up in groups, share the poem with the whole class, distribute copies of the poem to everyone, choose the student facilitator, and then have the discussion. I like to allow at least five minutes at the end of the session for the facilitator or another group member to share a few comments that summarize or characterize the overall experience.

To formally end the session, I offer some feedback about what I saw or heard, trying to bring us back to the poem itself as the lasting impression of the experience. "I can see that a poem like this one—'I Do Not Like My Father Much'—has caused intense reactions in many of us, myself included. I'm gratified you found so much to comment on in this poem about Langston Hughes's relationship with his father." This type of statement reinforces the deep level of involvement poetry can elicit and validates for students that I appreciate the risks they take when they openly share personal reactions with their peers.

Managing Groups

I try to have groups stay together for several sessions (through three to four peer-led discussions or so) to give them time to mesh and develop as a team, but eventually I'll mix them up to get different dynamics going. I often allow students to choose their own groups for discussion, with one clear proviso in mind: no one must be left out of a group or students will relinquish the privilege of choosing groups on their own.

Now and then, we spend a bit of time tackling those prickly group issues that come up, such as a member being argumentative, chronically interrupting, or otherwise behaving inappropriately. In trying to find a solution, I initially work within the group that's having a problem. If we can't solve it at that level, I bring the issue in front of the entire class for possible solutions. Let's face it— not every student will operate within your parameters, no matter how fair and reasonable they are. Fortunately, the majority of students are enthusiastic and willing to comply with the guidelines because they enjoy the camaraderie and relative autonomy of responding to poetry in smaller groups with their peers. In fact, here's a look at some of their survey comments about this type of discussion format.

> I prefer this kind of discussion because I get to say more.
>
> There aren't as many people and I can think better because there's not as much noise.
>
> Too many people try to talk at the same time.

I can't hear everyone's ideas about poetry, only those in our small group.

I like fewer people, but we shouldn't interrupt each other.

I like that everyone participates and has a lot to say.

I like when we're by ourselves and answer our own questions.

We all like to talk at the same time about different points of view.

It's easier to say things in a small group.

Some people have nothing to say, so they don't take their turn.

I agree with every one of these students comments, as well as the ones a few pages back about whole-class discussion, which only goes to show that each type of discussion format—whole-class and peer-led—has both benefits and limitations. I like having both types of discussion as a way to satisfy student preferences, which then helps get as many students as possible involved in sharing personal responses.

Whichever format you choose for classroom discussion (and I hope you'll include both), consider Rosenblatt's recommendation to focus on aesthetic stance first—the lived-through experience of emotions, memories, prior knowledge, etc.—since it is often that approach that deepens engagement and personal connection. Once such engagement is established, students are more ready, and likely more willing, to shift to an efferent stance and discuss the cognitive aspects of a poem, such as theme, poet's style, figurative language, and other literary devices. By acting as the "critical choreographer in this dance between stances" (Holland & Shaw)—asking for an aesthetic response before an efferent one—we help students move through both primary and secondary layers of response, enabling them to engage with poetry in ever deepening ways.

EXTENDING THE RESPONSE

Poetry calls forth a "lived-through experience" in each of us, which leads to various types of personal response. Our initial responses to poetry, through reflective writing and group discussion, might very well inspire additional reflection and still further response. In this way, poetry is a stimulus for a wide range of extension activities in which students explore and expand their ideas in ways that deepen personal connections, foster engagement, and help meet academic standards at the same time. The following chapter explores some ways to extend the poetry experience of your students through a variety of activities.

CHAPTER FOUR

Our Turn to Create:

Favorite Activities
Inspired by Poetry

> *Poetry is as important as family and as often ignored until it's really needed.... Even the darkest poem has a glimmer of hope because someone is telling it. Like raising a child, you do your best with a poem for as long as it lets you, and then you send it out alone, hoping it will be able to fend for itself, make its way without harm, find someone to fall in love with it and bring it home.*
>
> ~ Antonio Vallone

Poetry is a genre that seems to elicit layer upon layer of personal response. In the previous chapter, I wrote about the two most common forms of response, reflective writing and class discussion of poetry. This chapter explores still other layers of response, the many ways in which we can invite students to interact with poetry in individually creative ways. Let's take a look at some of the results when student audiences are inspired by a particular poem or become enchanted with poetry in general.

GETTING STARTED

Not all students are budding poets, and they won't all want to be, but with a little encouragement and support, they can each be successful creating poetry. Admittedly, the first few times we dabble in writing poetry, we don't try anything too sophisticated or complex. Instead, I often introduce a structured format some students find helpful early on in writing poetry, one that taps into a topic students know best—themselves.

Name Poems

Name Poems use an acrostic-style format. The procedure is quite simple and easy to follow. First, the student's name is printed down the side of a page. Each letter can then be used to begin a descriptive phrase or set of words about the person. For example, Tom might write:

Total soccer fan
Offers help to friends
Meatloaf-eater extraordinaire

To address certain language arts standards, I have students use dictionaries and thesauruses in the search process. Depending on past experience with these reference books, students will either already know how to locate words to use or will need a brief lesson that explains and guides them through a few examples.

Though there are many ways to approach this style of poem, I have students write Name Poems in which they provide three adjectives for each letter of their name. (If certain letters appear more than once in a given name, I may require only one or two adjectives for the repeated letters.) The thesaurus is especially useful for this type of search as it gives both synonyms and antonyms. I might say, "Maybe you think you're brave, but your name doesn't have the letter *b* in it. Look under *brave* in the thesaurus to see if any of the synonyms begin with a letter that is in your name." We look and find words such as *courageous, daring, fearless, gutsy, heroic,* and *intrepid*—great alternatives for *brave* if a student's name includes the letter *c, d, f, g, h,* or *i*.

The guidelines for this activity are straightforward: (1) students have to understand and be able to explain the meaning of every adjective they select for their poem, and (2) each selected word has to be a true descriptor about themselves. And of course the words have to be spelled correctly. Kids get quite involved with this process and are often found searching a thesaurus for other interesting words, whether they use them in their Name Poem or not. The exercise builds vocabulary at every step. As one student said, "I didn't know there were so many words for *happy* in the world!" And it's another way students learn that writers aren't out there in a vacuum, that poets and authors have resources to help them find the right words to suit their needs. The following are two Name Poems created by intermediate students:

Patriotic, poet, Polish
Athletic, attractive, American
Talented, thoughtful, ten-year-old
Reader, runner, racer
Intelligent, ice cream fan, Irish
Courageous, Coke drinker, crablegs lover
Kid, kooky, kind

Lanky, loyal, lovable
Energetic, eager, encouraging
Adventurous, athletic, animal lover
Healthy, helpful, honest

Bio Poems: A Perennial Favorite

Another kind of structured poem is the always popular Bio Poem. The Bio Poem's predetermined format—11 lines of specific personal information—is easy to follow and fun to complete. The poem begins with one's first name and ends with the last. In between are lines that describe and reveal thoughts and feelings of the student/poet, such as "Who feels..." and "Who fears..." (See page 126 for complete Bio Poem format.) Once all the poems, including my own, are edited and completed, I type them up and create a book. The final page of the book is for autographs. Each student receives her own copy as a keepsake of the year we spent together. I make one laminated copy that includes small photos of each student placed next to his Bio Poem. This special copy remains in the classroom for future students to borrow and read. Here is one example of a Bio Poem:

TAIT

Independent, masculine, intelligent, accelerated
Relative of Tricia Taylor
Lover of girls, food, soccer, football
Who feels sad when a girl dumps me, lots of self-esteem,
    glad when my friends are happy
Who needs girlfriends, friends, family
Who gives love, clothes, money
Who fears heights, cancer, drugs and alcohol
Who would like to see God, my grandpa, USS Arizona
Resident of the State of Confusion

TAYLOR

Students enjoy reading Bio Poems from the past, especially those that have been written by older siblings. These "limited edition" collections make students eager to create their own versions. Bio Poems are popular and well received, easy to compose, and become personal favorites of many students.

"Who Am I?" Poems

After many years of writing Bio Poems with my students, I decided to freshen up the structure to provide a little variety. I kept the popular theme—"the self"—but designed a different format, one that would retain some of the features of the Bio Poem yet would challenge students in a new way. I was also mindful of addressing academic standards involving expressive writing, such as exploring vivid imagery, expanding one's vocabulary, mastering fundamentals of grammar, and understanding figurative language. With these in mind, I devised a format titled the "Who Am I?" Poem. Like Bio Poems, they provide sentence starters or blank spaces that students complete with an appropriate word or phrase. These include adjectives, verbs, nouns, and similes that require not only personal reflection but also a knowledge of grammar and literary devices. The sound and feel of a completed "Who Am I?" Poem is lyrical in nature. Read the following example to see what I mean (see page 127 for the format of the "Who Am I?" Poem).

I'm generous and humorous and clumsy.
I wonder and work and give.
I'm a lover, a friend, a sister.

I sound like a monkey being teased,
I feel like a crab without a shell,
I move like a steady stream,
and look like an annoying kid (I am).

I'm as sweet as a lemon,
and blue as a blueberry.

I know about what women want.
I wonder about what men want.

I wait to go to middle school.
I long for a great future.
I hope for a day of relaxation.
I dream of a devoted man.

My name is Genevieve R.

The broader scope of the "Who Am I?" format presents a different challenge than Bio Poems, yet both involve students in the process of writing poetry. There's nothing sacred, however, about the design of either format. The beauty of this approach is that you and your students can alter, add, revise, or create a totally new and unique version of this type of poetry. Involving students in the format design allows creativity to shine and fosters engagement in the writing process.

WRITING INSPIRED BY POETRY

Poetry is remarkable in so many ways. One of its greatest attributes is the way it stimulates ideas for written response. Because poetry appeals to the senses, to the emotions, to the intellect, and to the imagination, it is particularly effective in inspiring further creativity. The next few pages include some of my favorite writing activities, which are natural extensions of poems my students and I have enjoyed.

Family/Friend Poems

Several years ago, poet Janet Wong was a keynote speaker at the Virginia Hamilton Conference on Multicultural Literature for Youth, held annually at Kent State University. During one of the workshop/dialogue sessions, Wong talked about writing poetry and the influence of culture and ancestry on her work. The importance of family is evident in the following poem from her book *A Suitcase of Seaweed*:

QUILT

Our family
is a quilt

of odd remnants
patched together

in a strange
pattern,

threads fraying,
fabric wearing thin—

but made to keep
its warmth

even in bitter
cold.

At the workshop, Wong invited participants to create a similar poem for a friend or family member as a tribute to that person. The format was simple—use a simile or metaphor to capture the qualities of a person. "My mother is like a blanket—warm, comforting, and protective," one person wrote. "My sister is an eagle—able to soar above everything" was another.

Wong encouraged us to give these poems, if possible, to the person named in the poem. As several people shared their poems with the whole group, it was apparent that a range of emotions had been triggered. Some of us were visibly moved by the experience. I had thoughts of both my parents, one still alive, one no longer with us. I thought of a favorite aunt, a distant cousin, a forgotten childhood friend. I could see the possibilities in this simple poem for tapping into memories and impressions of relatives and friends, along with all the accompanying emotions. It seemed to be the type of poetry experience students of any age could understand and enjoy. After sharing Janet Wong's poem "Quilt" with intermediate students and reviewing similes and metaphors, I had them write their own versions of Family/Friend Poems; here are some examples of their work:

*My mother is like a book—always interesting and
I never know what will happen next.*

My mom is like the rain—peaceful, quiet, and soothing.

*My mom is like a fresh-baked brownie because
she is warm and sweet.*

My dad is like a star—bright and always shining.

My family is like a tree with many branches.

My brother is like a stone—bold and strong.

"Girls About Boys and Boys About Girls"

The anthology *I Feel a Little Jumpy Around You* (Nye & Janeczko, 1996) is a wonderful collection of poems featuring the work of men and women writers. The poems in this book are arranged in pairs that highlight the way male and female writers look at the world. Sometimes these views are similar, other times quite different. The energy or tension between these partnered poems is what makes them so appealing, and the wide range of subject matter and style makes this a suitable anthology for intermediate through high school students and beyond.

My intermediate students enjoyed the selected poems I shared; they were especially intrigued by the notion of companion views. Inspired by this concept, they asked if they could write a book of their own titled *Girls About Boys and Boys About Girls*. In it, each person's opinions, feelings, and impressions about the opposite sex would be revealed. Some groaned at the thought of having to think about this in a direct way and actually be expected to write it down in black-and-white. Nonetheless, they wasted little time getting started. In fact, some of those who seemed initially resistant were the same ones who approached this in the most intense way, as if to say, *Good! Here's my chance to tell you what I* really *think!* And then they did!

The high level of engagement with this extension activity attests to the importance of giving students choice in the classroom. Since the idea for this class book came from one of their peers, students were eager to contribute their voices to it. One student also designed the book's cover. As facilitator, I was responsible for proofreading and making editing suggestions, and having the book pages laminated and spiral-bound. Mostly, though, I got to sit back and watch the process unfold. The experience was first-rate.

Excerpts from Girls About Boys and Boys About Girls

FROM THE GIRLS

❀ Mostly I think that boys are annoying. I think boys need to pay attention in class.

❀ I think boys should find out their girlfriend's favorite gemstone before (!) they get married. That's a big clue, boys!

❀ I think boys think about sports more than their girlfriends (if they have one). I think you should pray that you find the right one.

❀ The main thing I don't like about boys is that some boys think they are better than girls which I don't think is right!!!

❀ The best things about boys are they usually have a good sense of humor, and if you like them they do whatever you want.

❀ I hate boys with big teeth.

❀ Most boys make me frustrated because they ask me too many questions.

FROM THE BOYS

❀ I like the nice girls better than the bossy ones.

❀ One thing I don't like is they use too much makeup.

❀ Girls are what I think are a waste of space, mean, and ruthless. Girls care too much about their nails, hair, and smelling good. Yuck!

❀ The thing I don't like about girls is they like jewelry and hate bugs.

❀ Five things I like about girls are that some are beautiful, and some are tidy. Most girls are challenging, smart, and generous.

❀ I love girls!! Girls make great wives.

❀ I really hate it when girls play with each other's hair. I mean, what the heck is up with that?!

Copy/Change Poems

There might be other labels for this type of writing, but what matters most is the high level of engagement in a Copy/Change activity. The premise is simple: a published, professionally written poem is used as a model or template by students from which to create their own version. Parts of the original poem are retained ("copied") while other parts or words are removed ("changed") in the process. Where words or phrases are removed, students fill in their own ideas. Many individual poems could work well for this exercise, but the one I've included here is another Judith Viorst poem, "If I Were in Charge of the World." I like Viorst's writing for many reasons, not the least of which is that she's extremely adept at capturing what's inside the heads and hearts of children and adolescents (and adults as well!). Much of her poetry puts us smack-dab in the middle of the complex process of growing up, having friends, being alive, and navigating the world of emotions. It's a jungle out there, and she writes about it for us! Here is Viorst's original poem:

IF I WERE IN CHARGE OF THE WORLD

If I were in charge of the world
I'd cancel oatmeal,
Monday mornings,
Allergy shots, and also
Sara Steinberg.

If I were in charge of the world
There'd be brighter night lights,
Healthier hamsters, and
Basketball baskets forty-eight inches lower.

If I were in charge of the world
You wouldn't have lonely.
You wouldn't have clean.
You wouldn't have bedtimes.
Or "Don't punch your sister."
You wouldn't even have sisters.

If I were in charge of the world
A chocolate sundae with whipped cream and nuts
*   would be a vegetable.*
All 007 movies would be G.
And a person who sometimes forgot to brush,
And sometimes forgot to flush,
Would still be allowed to be
In charge of the world.

Viorst's poem is well suited to the Copy/Change activity because it names a host of things she would change in the world (if only she were in charge) that can be readily substituted with individual examples. For this extension activity, I first had students take turns reading the poem in pairs or small groups. They used expressive voices to convey just the right tone for the content of this poem, which helped prepare them for the writing activity that followed. Some students know just what it's like to get allergy shots or how it feels to be lonely. Because they can relate to so many of the ideas in the original, filling in the blanks—the "change" part of the poem—came more easily.

To make it easy for students to follow line by line, I made copies of the original and also created a formatted copy of the poem with blanks in selected places for them to complete. Guidelines were fairly straightforward. Students were to replace a missing word or phrase with a reasonably parallel substitution. In the line "I'd cancel <u>oatmeal</u>," for example, the word *oatmeal* had to be replaced with the name of a food, *Monday morning* with another day of the week/time of day, and so on. It's an enticing way to play with vocabulary, parts of speech, writing conventions, and rhyme scheme. When all student versions were written, we made a laminated class book that became a frequently borrowed item during independent reading. The words and phrases underlined in the following composite version of the poem show typical changes made by students.

If I were in charge of the world
I'd cancel <u>asparagus</u>,
<u>Sunday church</u>,
<u>Throat swabs</u>, and also
<u>Adolf Hitler</u>.

If I were in charge of the world
There'd be <u>all-girls' schools</u>,
<u>Smarter puppies</u>, and
<u>Home run walls 30 feet closer</u>.

If I were in charge of the world
You wouldn't have <u>sadness</u>.
You wouldn't have <u>chores</u>.
You wouldn't have <u>manners</u>.
Or "<u>Don't get bad grades.</u>"
You wouldn't even have <u>grades</u>.

If I were in charge of the world
A <u>Hostess Ho-Ho</u>
    would be a vegetable.
All "<u>too scary</u>" movies would be G.
And a person who sometimes forgot to <u>read</u>,
And sometimes forgot to <u>do a good deed</u>,
Would still be allowed to be
In charge of the world.

Students loved reading their Copy/Change poems to each other in pairs or to the entire class. They were especially gratified to see their versions made into a book that they or future classes could read.

To-Do Lists

This is one of those extension activities that evolved naturally following a poetry-sharing experience that caught our attention and imaginations in an unusual way. It was unplanned and somehow more satisfying because of the unexpected way it came about. It began one morning when I read a few poems from one of my poetry anthologies, *I Feel a Little Jumpy Around You* (Nye & Janeczko, 1996). Paging through the book, I found one titled "Emily Dickinson's To-Do List" by Andrea Carlisle. We had recently shared and discussed some of Dickinson's poetry, though I had not talked much about her life, with its many eccentricities. With Carlisle's poem in front of me, the opportunity was ripe for sharing some interesting details about the poet. In fact, this is a poem that would fall flat on its face and be virtually meaningless without essential background information to support one's understanding. Some of the pertinent facts about Emily Dickinson's life are in the box below. With this knowledge, you and your students will be able to understand and enjoy the poem that follows.

Essential Facts About Emily Dickinson's Life

❄ Emily lived her entire life in her parents' home in Amherst, Massachusetts. Neither she nor her prettier, younger sister, Lavinia (Vinnie), ever married.

❄ Emily loved simple pleasures and was especially fond of nature, flowers, and other living things.

❄ Though always painfully shy, Emily was considered witty and fun to be with once people got to know her.

❄ She began to write poetry in her teens, yet her family was unimpressed or uninterested in her writing.

❄ When a close friend and possible suitor, Ben Newton, died suddenly, Emily began to write poems about death, a common theme in her poetry for the rest of her life.

❄ Emily became increasingly reclusive and by the age of 40 almost never left home. (She did, however, like to eavesdrop when visitors came to call.)

❄ Around this same time, Emily began to wear only white.

❄ Considered a skillful and talented cook, Emily often made gifts of gingerbread and other treats for her brother Austin and his wife, Sue, who lived next door.

❄ Emily had an ongoing correspondence with Thomas Wentworth Higginson, an essayist and man of letters from whom she initially sought advice about her poems.

❄ Baffled by her startling originality, which did not conform to then-current notions of poetry, Higginson advised Emily to delay publication but encouraged her to continue writing.

❄ During her lifetime, only a handful of Emily's poems were published.

❄ After Emily's death at age 56, Lavinia found hundreds of her poems tied up in packets and hidden away in a dresser drawer.

❄ Though her family and friends knew she wrote poetry, they had never realized the extent of her talent.

EMILY DICKINSON'S TO-DO LIST
Sum-Sum-Summertime

Monday

Figure out what to wear—white dress?

Put hair in bun

Bake gingerbread for Sue

Peer out window at passersby

Write poem

Hide poem

Tuesday

White dress? Off-white dress?

Feed cats

Chat with Lavinia

Work in garden

Letter to T.W.H.

Wednesday

White dress or what?

Eavesdrop on visitors from behind door

Write poem

Hide poem

Thursday

Try on new white dress

*Gardening—watch out for narrow
    fellows in grass!*

Gingerbread, cakes, treats

Poems: Write and hide them

Friday

Embroider sash for white dress

Write poetry

Water flowers on windowsill

Hide everything

This is a lovely poem—witty and clever—and when I read it, my students soon realized the importance of the background information our prior discussion provided. Carlisle took what she knew of Dickinson's life, idiosyncrasies, habits, and talents and wrote from that point of view. The poem gave us a glimpse of Emily's personality through a delightfully creative form—a to-do list—which captured the essence of her personality and behavior in a succinct and sympathetic way.

After a satisfying class discussion of the poem, I wondered aloud how interesting it would be to write someone else's to-do list, the way Carlisle did for Dickinson. My students were eager to try it, so we decided to use *me* as the subject. First, we reviewed the concept of point of view and what we need to know when taking on the views and personality of another: their likes and dislikes, aspects of their character, their behavior patterns, the way they talk or act, and what others might say or think about them. Then, stepping into *my* point of view, students volunteered ideas for "Mrs. Perfect's To-Do List." The following is a partial list of those ideas:

1. *Work on book draft.*
2. *Pack chocolate*
3. *Go on walk; find birds of prey.*

4. *Stock up on hand grenades to clean desk at school.*
5. *Give Noah a "noogie."*
6. *Convince Ryan to share his popcorn.*
7. *Pout/beg kids for airline tickets.*
8. *Make fun of school lunch.*
9. *Hate recess duty; pray for rain.*
10. *Go home, talk about annoying day with kids.*
11. *Make reservations for dinner.*
12. *Give "antidisestablishmentarianism" as bonus spelling word.*
13. *Tell girls the importance of devoted boys.*
14. *Say "Please go away so I can miss you" to an annoying student.*
15. *Look for more good poetry books.*

I finally had to stop the list at 40-something, but what a treat it was to hear myself being revealed in this activity! This list showed my students to be incredibly perceptive and accurate. They knew me inside and out, that's for sure, and had done an excellent job of capturing my quirks, opinions, and personality. It was almost scary.

"Mrs. Perfect's To-Do List" was a group effort, but now it was time to write one of their own. Each student selected someone other than themselves, someone they knew well so they could write from that person's point of view. The results were wonderful and satisfying and ranged from To-Do Lists for parents, siblings, and best friends (or enemies!) to ones for pets. Here's a partial list one student wrote about his best friend.

Go to school and make up jokes.
Make drawings of funny stuff.
Almost miss bus.
Tell Mrs. Perfect the word "strangle" in Italian.

Another student wrote from her older sister's point of view.

Yell at little sister for no reason whatsoever.
Complain about all the chores I have to do.
Complain about mom's cigarette smoke.

CHARACTER STUDY

In addition to To-Do Lists, students could write character sketches of someone in a poem. Consider poems such as "The Cremation of Sam McGee" by Robert Service or "The Road Not Taken" by Robert Frost. What do these poems reveal about the main character? What can we guess about them from the poet's words? What specific clues do we find about this person in the poem? Think of still other possibilities for extension activities involving character study and point of view. Locate poems that will support this type of writing exercise, or other similar activities that will help students master related academic standards.

Change clothes 3 times before school in the morning
   (even though I look fine).
Go "Mo-o-om!" every time she won't let me do something.
Go "Eeeeee!" every time Matt T. walks by.

The following ideas are from a To-Do List for the family's cat.

Sleep on chair.
Sleep on couch.
Sleep on Noah's bookbag.
Sleep in basket.
Sleep on TV.
Visit litter box.

In writing their To-Do Lists, students demonstrated a clear understanding of point of view, a concept typically examined through other genres of literature, such as fiction or expository text. But Carlisle's poem about Emily Dickinson, a powerful example of point-of-view writing, illustrates that character can be explored and revealed in creative ways through poetry as well.

"How to Scratch an Itch"

Every year, Arnold Adoff becomes one of my students' favorite poets. His poetry, which often sounds like jazz riffs when read aloud, always delights the mind and ear. Adoff's work covers a broad spectrum of themes and subjects and includes such volumes as *Eats*, *The Basket Counts*, and *Love Letters*. In one of his most recent books, *Touch the Poem*, I found this poem about a common dilemma and knew it would bring smiles to my class.

FIVE WAYS TO BE ALONE
WITH AN ITCH IN THE CENTER OF MY BACK

1. Rub Myself On The Corner Of The Hallway Wall.
2. Roll On The Family Room Carpet.
3. Scratch Myself With The Kitchen Broom Handle.
4. Scratch Myself With The Kitchen Broom.
5. Drop The Cat Down My Shirt.

I read the poem again more slowly and asked students to imagine using each technique mentioned in the poem to scratch an itch of their own. They especially loved the crazy but likely very effective No. 5 on Adoff's list. At the end of the second reading my students were "itching" to add their own ideas to his. Every student's hand went up, waving for recognition. The ideas tumbled out one after the other and I could barely keep up as I scribbled their ideas on chart paper. When the page was full, the ideas were still coming, so I had them take a few minutes to write their remaining suggestions on their own papers. The box below shows some of them.

shish kebab skewer	tip of Mount Everest	bottom of golf shoes
popsicle stick	football cleats	eraser end of a pencil
leaf rake	my sister's toothbrush	bark of a tree
radio antenna	scissors	hairbrush
yardstick	elephant tusk	foot of a Barbie doll
carrot	screwdriver	chainsaw
porcupine	fork	banana

This kind of enthusiastic response is commonplace when students are frequently immersed in poetry. From a simple poem springs spontaneous extension activities that are often unplanned and unexpected but almost always satisfying. This particular experience was quick, short, and engaging— and every single student was involved in the list-making process that emerged from reading the poem.

GRAPHIC AND CREATIVE ARTS

Discussion and written expression activities, aren't the only ways to respond to poetry. Because poetry is itself a creative art, this genre is well-suited to other artistic forms of response. See if any of the following ideas might work with some of the poetry you share with students.

Illustration

Certain poems are especially conducive to artistic representation. Students who are talented and creative in this way, or are willing to try graphic renderings, enjoy the chance to capture their impressions of a poem or the memories evoked by a poem in drawings, paintings, and other visual art forms. Poetry with vivid images or about the world of nature—the poems in *Cactus Poems* (Frank Asch), for example—seems especially conducive to student artwork.

Photographic Exploration

Imagine the interesting and creative results if we could put a disposable camera in the hands of every student and ask them to capture photo images of what a poem meant to them. Consider using the e.e. cummings poem "in Just-spring" or "The Red Wheelbarrow" by William Carlos Williams for this kind of photographic exploration. The possibilities for this type of interpretive response are wide open.

Container Poetry (Dioramas)

One of the most popular and successful activities my students have done with poetry is creating a dioramalike scene to depict their impressions of a self-selected poem. I call it Container Poetry since the students choose a box, basket, jar, or other container in which to create and showcase their three-dimensional representation. The idea for this came from a poetry workshop I took at a local university several years ago taught by Dr. Carolyn Brodie. It was one of the highlights of that class. In the years since, students have always been eager to do this activity and have especially enjoyed when other classes visit to see their finished projects.

Dramatic Interpretation

Every now and then, a particular poem is ready-made for dramatic or physical interpretation. Shel Silverstein's "Crowded Tub" is one of our class favorites. We put a little action behind each line as we recite the poem together.

Adding gestures or other physical movements seems to increase enjoyment of certain poems. This type of physical involvement also helps students memorize the lines of a poem at the same time it dramatizes it. But though it has its place from time to time, dramatic interpretation can be tricky: you can try things out with younger students that you would never attempt with older ones. Your decisions about when to use dramatic interpretation or physical movement with poetry will be based on the grade level or age of your students. Used appropriately and judiciously, dramatization becomes one more way to explore creative response to poetry.

Poetry Quilt

One of the most rewarding poetry experiences my students and I have had was the year we created a Poetry Quilt as a lasting keepsake of our time together. That year was special for many reasons. These were students I had taught for two consecutive years in a looping experience, and they also were participants in a qualitative study for my doctoral dissertation involving student response to poetry. Making a Poetry Quilt was one of those ideas that comes into your head when you can't sleep in the middle of the night. At least, that's when this project started to take shape. When I shared the "midnight inspiration" with my class, they were as enthusiastic as I was.

The basic plan was fairly simple: each student would choose a poem or poet they liked and make a drawing depicting their vision of that poem that would become one of the squares of a Poetry Quilt. The only restriction was that no two students could select the same poem or poet— but with the vast array of options, that was not a concern. Each drawing was done on a ten-inch square of paper, which I then used as my pattern for cutting the student's drawing into pieces, tracing onto fabric, and sewing each piece together to form the "picture" using an appliqué technique. Once each appliquéd square was completed, the name of the poem and poet was printed along the top edge. Each student signed his/her name along the bottom edge. Yes, the Poetry Quilt was a project that took many dozens of hours of time to complete, but it stands as a testimony to the joy we experienced and the love we developed for poetry of all kinds.

PERFORMING WITH POETRY

Poetry in its written form is only half awake. When we bring it off the page and read it aloud, it comes fully alive for ourselves and others to enjoy. Here are some possibilities you might enjoy for sharing poetry aloud.

Daily Student Poetry Share

At some point in the year—sometimes weeks, sometimes months into it—after students are immersed in my daily reading of poetry, they begin to ask if they, too, could read a poem they've found to the class. This is always a wonderful thing. I have several expectations: students must practice reading it aloud (on their own) so they're comfortable with it and can pronounce all the words, and they must read fluently and loud enough for all to hear. Some students prefer to read with a partner or small group, and it's always interesting to hear the way they've decided which lines to read singly, which lines together, and so on. I encourage this kind of collaboration for oral reading of poetry as it provides a safer forum for those students who want to try it but are a little tentative about being alone up there with an audience looking on. Then there's always the brave ones from the get-go—some students who are naturals at finding just the right tone of voice, the right pitch, the right emphasis—as if the genre of poetry were waiting for them to bring it to the rest of us. What a thrill it is when this happens!

Once students express the desire to read poetry to the class, it's important to establish a specific time of day for it to happen. With my intermediate students, I designated a 10- to 15-minute slot right after lunch each day. In the middle school setting, such sharing worked best on most days at the beginning or end of a Reading or Language Arts period or on given days of the week. Remember that a poem takes very little time to read, and it may spark a livelier discussion or written response activity than what you had planned. Each teacher's decision about when to have a poetry share will be determined by grade level, schedule, class environment, and other such variables.

Group Performances and Choral Reading

Some poems are perfectly suited for whole-class participation, and Jack Prelutsky's "Bleezer's Ice Cream" is one of them. Essentially, this poem is a list of alliterative, tongue-twisting, obnoxious-sounding ice cream flavors one could find at Bleezer's Ice Cream Store, such as:

COCOA MOCHA MACARONI
TAPIOCA SMOKED BALONEY
BUTTER BRICKLE PEPPER PICKLE
POMEGRANATE PUMPERNICKEL

Not only is the poem fun to say with all its tongue twists and tangles, it also provides an opportunity to perform a delightful poem for other classes. Students can form a large circle around the edges of a classroom and take turns reading each disgusting flavor. Individual lines of the poem can be printed out and put on ice-cream-cone shapes, with each student holding a cone and reading her respective flavor. The first and last stanzas of the poem can be read by a designated "narrator." The performance of this poem takes only a few minutes of time, involves virtually no "props" (other than the lines printed on ice-cream-cone shapes), and demands no rearrangement of classroom furniture or students. Quick. Easy. Delightful all around!

Poetry Café

When you bring poetry to students on a regular basis, they can hardly resist falling for it and wanting more. And if you also have students who like to read it aloud themselves (as discussed above) or listen to their classmates read, you've got the right situation for planning a Poetry Café. This popular activity has been around awhile and written about in books and magazines such as *Instructor*. Based on the coffeehouses of the 1950s and 1960s (and the current resurgence of these as well), a Poetry Café takes place in a classroom transformed into a café—dim lights, refreshments such as chips or cookies and punch or soda, groups of desks pushed together as "tables" and covered with tablecloths, jazz music playing in the background. The idea is to create an ambience for enjoying poetry. Everybody dresses like a "beat poet"—in a black beret and turtleneck or similar garb. But the main feature, of course, is the reading and reciting of poetry. Students select a favorite poem to share, either read it from a book or recite it from memory, and simply soak in the atmosphere surrounding them. Instead of clapping, we snap our fingers in applause for each "performer." Someone mans the bongo drums for extra emphasis between readings. Loving poetry and having some fun with it is the point of this activity.

Poetry Celebrations and Events

The ways to celebrate and feature poetry in your instruction are limitless. Some teachers like to feature poetry in a special way during National Poetry Month, which is April. Even if you share poetry regularly throughout the year, showcasing poetry in April (or any other segment of time, for that matter) gives you the chance to involve students in performing for other classes or parents, creating hallway displays, making bulletin boards, designing a poetry collage or mural, researching individual poets and reporting on them, or doing an in-depth study focused on a particular poet. Posters celebrating poetry can be found on certain Web sites free or at minimal cost and can be a nice way to augment your teaching and planned activities. Teachers' catalogs are also good resources in which to find posters and bulletin board displays that highlight poetry in some way. Students can always be counted on to design original poetry posters or bookmarks or bumper stickers or—well, you get the idea. Bring them the poetry, help them learn to love it, and the celebration becomes a natural extension of the process.

WRITING ORIGINAL POETRY

One of the first signs that my students are becoming hooked on the genre of poetry is a noticeable increase in the number of poetry books checked out of our school library. Or I might start to see a good handful of students choose a volume of poetry for self-selected reading time. More and more often, individuals or groups of students ask to read poetry aloud to the class. And sooner or later after frequent exposure to poetry in the classroom, students seem to want to try their own hand at writing poetry, which they do both on their own and during writing workshop. Early attempts are admirable but usually less than stellar. While students need to be praised for their eager desire to write poetry, they also need to be gently but firmly guided toward revision, an important step in the process. This is where the "teachable moment" enters the room. I confer with students about their original poetry. Often, their work suggests a mini-lesson that would benefit the class as a whole, and I ask permission to use the work as a model for revision.

Since my reaction to their poem is respectful and enthusiastic, most students are quite willing to have me use their first draft this way. Let me offer some general guidelines regarding poetry revisions, followed by a more detailed example of how the process unfolds.

Guiding Students Toward Revision

When students begin to write original poetry, either on their own or as a class activity, it's important to praise their early work. I want them to feel proud of their efforts, but I also want them to be willing to continue the writing process—editing, revising, and rewriting. I remind them that most writing improves with revision, yet this is usually the step that many writers (myself included) balk at. Teachers need a fair amount of finesse in convincing students to persevere in their writing (of anything, not just poetry!) without turning them off along the way. To do this, I try to be at least twice as complimentary as I am critical about the work or the potential in it. I also try to keep student writing in perspective, being supportive and positive about it, while remembering we are *all* developing as writers every day. Progress, not perfection.

One Monday morning, Julianne, an articulate, creative fourth grader, brought me this "poem" that she'd written over the weekend.

THE SKY

There up high in the sky lay
the fluffy white and gray clouds.
When you look up in the sky you
use your imagination and you
can see clouds shaped like animals.
You can see birds flapping their
Wings very softly in the wind.

A lot of sad weather comes from
the sky like rain, snow, hail, thunder
and lightning. Some small children
are afraid that the sky may fall some
day. Most adults know the sky can't
fall. It will stay up there in it's cold
airless atmosphere.

~ Julianne C.

This "poem" looked and sounded more like prose than poetry. Though I was genuinely excited at Julianne's desire to write a poem and her worthy effort, false or overdone praise serves neither the young poet nor the cause of poetry well. So first comes the "good news." I picked examples of her words that I thought worked especially well for me and said, "I love some of your language. 'Sad weather' and 'airless atmosphere' really stand out for me." Then I asked what had inspired the poem, and she said "I just thought of it!" as if poetry is a natural outcome of an idea or strong feelings that come to mind. She is right! This is often true, and I told her so, affirming her effort. "That is just how many poets get started—an idea just comes to them. I'm glad you took the time to act upon your inspiration. That's the first step. Now we can take some time to work with your good ideas."

First, I reminded Julianne of the way poetry often looks on a page: "Remember how the lines in poems are often short, and sometimes have only a word or two? Poetry sounds and looks different from prose. Poets usually write with brief phrases, using only the most important and meaningful words." Then I asked if she wanted me to work with her to arrange and revise the words to look and sound more like poetry than prose. She was eager to do so. As we collaborated for roughly 10 to 15 minutes, our dialogue went something like this:

ME: "When you read the poem out loud, it sounds a lot like a paragraph, don't you think?"

JULIANNE: "Yes, I guess it does sound like that."

ME: "I'm wondering if we could go through your poem and remove some words that aren't necessary to get your point across. We could also put fewer words on each line to look more like poetry."

JULIANNE: "Let's do that because I want it to look like a poem and sound like a poem."

As we began to go through her work line by line, I suggested which words could be removed. For example, in this line from the original version: "When you look up in the sky you use your imagination and you can see clouds shaped like animals…," we took away some words, put fewer words on a line, and the result looked and sounded better: "Look up/in the sky/Let your imagination/see clouds shaped like animals." Julianne liked this change, and was beginning to see how specific revisions, such as more concise wording and different placement of line breaks, could improve her poem. After going through a few of these lines, she took a more active part in editing her poem with suggestions like the following:

JULIANNE: "Where I wrote 'You can see birds flapping their wings very softly in the wind,' I could change that to 'See birds flapping their wings/softly in the wind.'"

ME: (nodding my head enthusiastically) "You're beginning to see how a poet plays with words, using fewer rather than more. I also like your choices about where you want your reader to take a breath or pause by putting line breaks in different places."

We continued revising in this manner until the entire poem was rewritten. Here is the second version of Julianne's poem:

THE SKY

There up high
*   in the sky*
lay fluffy
white and gray clouds.
Look up
*   in the sky*
Let your imagination
*   see clouds shaped like animals.*
See birds flapping their wings
*   softly in the wind.*

Sad weather comes—
*   rain, snow, hail, thunder,*
lightning.
Small children are afraid
*   the sky may fall some day.*
Adults know the sky won't fall.
The sky will stay
up in its cold
airless
atmosphere.

Julianne was both proud and pleased with the poem she created. And so was I. I also saw how useful her work could be in showing her classmates various aspects of the changes involved when revising a poem. At my request, she was willing to share her first draft and the improved second version with the rest of the class in a whole-group mini-lesson on the revision process. The following is a brief summary of what took place.

Mini-Lesson on the Revision Process

Julianne's classmates were especially attentive during the revision mini-lesson and the discussion that followed. As her peers, I think they appreciated the risk she was taking in allowing her work to be "out there" for public scrutiny. To get us started, I passed out copies of Julianne's first and second versions of the poem, printed side by side, so everyone could see the changes we had made. She and I took a few minutes to tell the rest of the class how the revision process evolved between us, pointing out some of the specific changes that occurred as a result of our collaboration. Once they saw firsthand how much better Julianne's second version looked and sounded than the first, they were noticeably impressed with her writing process.

After briefly discussing what had already been changed, the class and I decided to continue the polishing process with Julianne's poem. Many of the issues we focused on were similar to the ones she and I had discussed earlier in our initial revision.

It was gratifying that students were serious about the revision process and, at the same time, so supportive of Julianne's work. The following student comments show their awareness of the features of poetry and careful attention to details.

❋ I think Julianne ought to change the lines about "small children being afraid" and "adults knowing the sky won't fall" because the poem is about what you see in the sky, and not about kids being afraid of it. It gets off track in that part, I think.

❋ I wonder if the word *imagination* has too many syllables in it. Could that word be changed to *mind* or something like that to make the rhythm flow better?

❋ Those weather words—*rain, snow, hail, thunder, lightning*—maybe they should all be one-syllable words so they match better. (revision: "rain, snow, hail, fog")

❋ Maybe she could add a couple more places at the end where some words rhymed since she has a little of that in the beginning.

❋ Since Julianne repeats the words *in the sky* a few times, I think she should have that as the title of the poem.

What began as a mini-lesson turned into so much more. Our class discussion of Julianne's poem was a marvelous collaboration of voices that resulted in her making several revisions. Much was learned in the process. This is Julianne's final version:

IN THE SKY

There up high
> *in the sky*
lay fluffy
white and gray clouds.
Look up
> *in the sky,*
Let your mind
> *see animal clouds.*

In the sky
> *wings of birds*
> *softly flap*
>> *in the wind.*

Sad weather comes—
> *rain, snow, hail, fog.*
Every day
> *the sky will stay*
in its cold and
> *airless*
> *atmosphere.*

Throughout this process, Julianne's confidence in her work never wavered. Her own voice was a vital part of the class discussion, and she was gracious and agreeable as others suggested changes. "You're the poet," I told her, "so you have the right to accept or reject any of our ideas." And in fact, she did some of both. Her poem, shared first in a mini-lesson, revised as a group, then displayed where all could see it, made some of her classmates eager to write their own poetry as well. The steps we took in this poetry revision can be followed in most cases of original student writing:

1. Determine if a student is ready.

2. Provide positive feedback.

3. Offer suggestions based on key features of poetry: rhyme, rhythm, line breaks, and so on.

4. Be specific as you suggest/model possible revisions.

5. Guide the student into changes he or she is comfortable with.

6. Allow the student to decide on what to keep or change.

7. Celebrate the completed revision in some way: displaying the work, adding it to a student's portfolio, sharing it aloud with the class, etc.

ALWAYS AN ADVENTURE

There is almost no end to the kinds of creative activities poetry inspires. Even a single poem holds so many possibilities. In this chapter, I took a brief look at some of the ways students have explored the genre of poetry either through writing original poetry or extending a poem to another place based on what it says to them and where it invites them to go. The next chapter moves into another exciting realm—bringing poetry into every area of the curriculum—which is like throwing open a window to let in fresh air.

CHAPTER FIVE

Making Content Come Alive:

Integrating Poetry Into the Content Areas

Students develop a love of poetry when teachers use it wisely as a natural part of every day. . . . As teachers, we can experience the joy of giving poetry to another generation of children, expanding their language and enriching their lives. We benefit, too, because we cannot give beauty to children without the scent of roses clinging to our hands.

~ Bernice E. Cullinan

In the previous chapter, I offered various poetry formats to get kids writing their own poetry as well as ideas for extension activities for individual poems. But while poetry can stand on its own and often does, it can also be brought into other areas of the curriculum to help content-area topics become more meaningful, more concrete, and more alive for students.

Poetry is one of the most accessible of all genres, making it a practical choice for instruction. Because it is written about virtually any topic imaginable, poetry can be found to introduce, emphasize, advance, or enhance any subject or theme you have in mind. When poetry is used as a bridge to content-area topics, a whole new dimension of understanding and appreciation develops. Poems have "the potential to capture the ear, imagination, and souls of their listeners" (Lenz, 1992). When was the last time you noticed that kind of attention given to, say, science texts or math books? Poetry doesn't mean to replace as much as augment and support other resources or texts used in teaching these subjects.

Poetry helps build a framework for deeper learning and can be used "to broaden the knowledge base and motivate children to learn in other areas of the curriculum" (Myers, 1997–98). A carefully selected poem can infuse life and energy into the sometimes dry, technical content-area subjects such as math, science, or social studies. In social studies, for example, poetry can help build a conceptual background and understanding of other people—their customs, beliefs, and lifestyles. When students use this understanding to also make personal connections and comparisons, their interest and engagement with the topic of study increases.

A study by McClure and Zitlow (1991) focused on the way poetry can capture "the aesthetic aspects of the scientific phenomena" and, in doing so, make science more meaningful to students. On the importance of bringing aesthetic and efferent response together, they wrote:

> Nowhere is the aesthetic dimension more neglected than in the content area subjects—science, social studies, and mathematics. Concern for teaching the facts has caused us to neglect forging an emotional connection between those facts and the lives of our children. Adding the aesthetic dimension, through literature and *particularly poetry* [*emphasis added*], can help students look beyond the facts to discover the beauty and richness that lies within a subject.

There are limitless ways to bring poetry into your instruction and make it a part of any subject of the curriculum. In the rest of this chapter, you'll find suggestions for using poetry in various content-area subjects, including what to do with individual poems and poetry books, based on what has worked well in my own classroom. As you read, think of other ways to include poetry in your teaching and specific activities or extensions that spring from the poems you select.

Anthologies for Integrating Poetry into the Curriculum

Americans' Favorite Poems: The Favorite Poem Project Anthology, edited by Robert Pinsky and Maggie Dietz

A Child's Anthology of Poetry, edited by Elizabeth Hauge Sword

Classic Poems to Read Aloud, selected by James Berry

The Invisible Ladder: An Anthology of Contemporary American Poems for Young Readers, edited by Liz Rosenberg

Poetry 180: A Turning Back to Poetry, selected by Billy Collins

The Random House Book of Poetry for Children, selected by Jack Prelutsky

Read-Aloud Poems for Young People, edited by Glorya Hale

Sing a Song of Popcorn: Every Child's Book of Poems, selected by Beatrice Schenck de Regniers et al.

Talking Like the Rain, selected by X. J. Kennedy and Dorothy M. Kennedy

POETRY AND MATH

Shel Silverstein's poem "Smart," from *Where the Sidewalk Ends,* is an example of how accessible and fun poetry can be as part of a lesson on subtraction and money values. In this poem, a dad gives his son a one-dollar bill, who then makes a series of trades that leave him with more coins but less money. Kids are delighted to practice subtraction skills either with paper and pencil or in their minds as they follow the text of the poem. Older students could also engage in discussion about character study, using clues from the poem to make inferences about the son and his father, their relationship, and their individual personalities.

The poem "Arithmetic" by Carl Sandburg is written in free verse and offers great imagery as it poses a few interesting dilemmas in dealing with numbers. The imaginative wordplay is highly engaging and gives students a chance to speculate on possible answers to the questions raised.

from ARITHMETIC

Arithmetic is where numbers fly
like pigeons in and out of your head.
Arithmetic tells you how many you lose or win
if you know how many you had
before you lost or won.
Arithmetic is seven eleven all good children
go to heaven—or five six bundle of sticks.
Arithmetic is numbers you squeeze from your
head to your hand to your pencil to your paper
till you get the right answer. . . .
If you have two animal crackers, one good and one bad,
and you eat one and a striped zebra
with streaks all over him eats the other,
how many animal crackers will you have
if somebody offers you five six seven and you say
No no no and you say Nay nay nay
and you say Nix nix nix?
If you ask your mother for one fried egg
for breakfast and she gives you
two fried eggs and you eat
both of them, who is better in arithmetic,
you or your mother?

Students may be asked to write an answer to the question posed in the last few lines and give persuasive reasons for their response. Similarly, using Sandburg's poem as a model, they could write original descriptions of arithmetic or math using vivid imagery that appeals to the senses. Students could work in small groups to create a list of the importance of numbers in their lives, perhaps putting their ideas in categories such as home, school, sports, relationships, and so on.

A number of books are available that focus entirely on math concepts. One such book is *Arithme-tickle: An Even Number of Odd Riddle-Rhymes* by J. Patrick Lewis. This collection is just what it claims—a delightful set of brainteasers using not only math skills but also general knowledge about various subjects. Here's an excerpt from one of them to show you what I mean:

A REGULAR RIDDLE

What's the number of points on a regular star,
Less the number of wheels on a regular car,
Plus the number of teeth in a regular mouth,
Less the number of states that begin with South. . . .

Some of these poems require paper and pencil to solve (and maybe another resource book or two, depending on the grade level); others can be done using mental math. The riddles involve a variety of math concepts (odd and even numbers, multistep problems using addition and subtraction, distance, time, money) and knowledge of math terminology (*sum, perpendicular, average*). They can be solved individually, in small groups, or as a whole class. Since saying each "riddle-rhyme" is part of the fun, my class enjoys the small- or whole-group approach in solving the riddles. But they know accurate math calculations count, too.

A simple extension activity would be to select one of the riddle-rhymes to use as a model, then write originals and create a class collection. This is a lighthearted way to blend poetry with math concepts without feeling like it's "work."

POETRY AND SCIENCE

Though each grade level has specific science units or themes to cover during that year, finding poetry that connects well with science topics is practically effortless. Think of some of the major categories science includes: nature, the earth, astronomy, weather, oceans, landforms, living things, electricity, inventions, machines, the human body, nutrition, and on and on it goes. Here are just a few ideas for linking poetry with science topics.

When I taught intermediate grades, one of the independent projects students completed in the fall was a leaf collection. As a way of introducing this project, I read poetry from *Old Elm Speaks: Tree Poems* by Kristine O'Connell George. I remember quite vividly the way students relaxed into the poetry, "seeing" trees in a different light, enjoying the imagery brought forth in the poems. The following poem was one of their favorites:

AUTUMN

All summer long,
trees studied the sun
to learn the secret
of her fire.

First, they practiced
tracing sunset rays
along their ribs
in colors remembered
from hot summer days.

Now, their chance
on center stage—
they rage yellow gold red,
setting the hills ablaze.

Another wonderful and recently published book is *The Blood-Hungry Spleen and Other Poems About Our Parts* by Allan Wolf. I included the poem "Spit" from this collection in Chapter One; here's an excerpt from another:

SHY SILENT RIVERS

. . . Arteries rush the blood away
to hungry cells in every part.
Every port. Distant limbs.
Tributaries. Tiny slivers.
Oxygen, food, and life to deliver.
Shy red silent rivers . . .

This has become one of the more popular books on my poetry shelf. Students clamor to borrow it whenever they can, often choosing one or more of them to read aloud to their classmates during poetry sharing time. This poetry collection makes the human body more than just an obligatory unit of study. Because they are cleverly (and sometimes irreverently) written, the poems make the topic "come alive" in a way most informational science texts do not. They delight and inform at the same time. Wolf's poems are written and organized into various categories, including the few shown below:

* "That's You All Over" (skin)
* "On the Face of It" (face, nose, eyes, ears, lips, tongue, teeth)
* "Parts That Bend" (fingers, toes, knees, elbows, ankles)
* "A Bone (or Two) to Pick with You" (skeletal system)
* "Bellybuttons and Bottoms" (self-explanatory!)
* "The Circulation Department" (heart, arteries and veins, spleen)

Students can use science texts and poems together to find and list facts about the body or to write descriptive paragraphs using the details found in each resource.

The study of living things, particularly the animal kingdom, is wide open for including poetry to give it an extra punch. Skimming through the index of titles in *The Random House Book of Poetry for Children*, I found poems that could readily find their way into lessons on mammals, reptiles, birds, insects, arthropods, fish, and so on:

"The Alligator"	"Dragonfly"	"The Great Auk's Ghost"
"Brontosaurus"	"The Eagle"	"The Hedgehog"
"The Camel's Complaint"	"The Flea"	"I Had a Little Pig"

This is a list of poems from this one anthology alone, poems about animals for almost every letter of the alphabet. More are to be found in other collections. Here's one of Emily Dickinson's well-loved poems about a reptile.

A NARROW FELLOW IN THE GRASS

A narrow fellow in the grass
Occasionally rides;
You may have met him,—did you not,
His notice sudden is.

The grass divides as with a comb,
A spotted shaft is seen;
And then it closes at your feet
And opens further on.

He likes a boggy acre,
A floor too cool for corn.
Yet when a child, and barefoot,
I more than once, at morn,

Have passed, I thought, a whip-lash
Unbraiding in the sun,—
When, stooping to secure it,
It wrinkled, and was gone.

Several of nature's people
I know, and they know me;
I feel for them a transport
Or cordiality;

But never met this fellow,
Attended or alone,
Without a tighter breathing,
And zero at the bone.

Dickinson's poetry takes some adjusting to; the way she transposes words—"his notice sudden is"—and her innovative phrasing—"zero at the bone"—require a bit of attention. But what imaginative words and descriptions she uses to tell us her feelings about snakes! Whenever I share this poem, my students like the way the poet does not come right out and call this creature a snake or reptile, but identifies it instead as "a narrow fellow in the grass," which they find more enchanting—and much more literary.

And here's one more take on the snake (sorry!), by Eve Merriam:

VIPER

Viper, viper
spiteful sniper,
snake in the grass, lowdown, base,
smiling, smiling to your face,
virulent villain, venomous, vile,
darting poison with a snaky smile.

Pure word fun! Grab the dictionaries and thesauruses and have a word search for other appropriate descriptors for snakes. And why stop there? Extend the activity over time to other living things that you study in science.

POETRY AND SOCIAL STUDIES

One of the best recent anthologies of poetry to celebrate America is by poet and anthologist Lee Bennett Hopkins. *My America: A Poetry Atlas of the United States* is a collection of poetry organized into eight sections—one for each region of the U.S. It begins with facts about the states of that region, such as capital city, nickname, state motto, and size in square miles. Part poetry, part atlas, this book is chock-full of images, impressions, and descriptions of every unique region represented. *My America* is a tribute to the greatness and diversity that make this country special. Perhaps a sampling from this book will convince you to acquire it and use it in your own classroom. Here is the opening stanza of a poem by Lillian M. Fisher that can be found in the section on the Southwest region:

DESERT

The desert is holding a giant breath
The air is dusty and dry
Red mesas shimmer in searing heat
Under a blanket of sky.

Or try this one by Patricia Hubbell from the Northeast region:

VERMONT CONVERSATION

"Good weather for hay."
"Yes, 'tis."
"Mighty bright day."
"That's true."

"Crops comin' on?"
"Yep. You?"
"Tol'rable; beans got the blight."
"Way o' the Lord."
"That's right."

This is a lovely collection featuring poetry from both past and contemporary poets. Their voices and their poems appeal to our senses as well as to our national pride. Everything about this book is attractive: the poems, the variety of poetry styles, the arrangement of poems into regions, and the interpretive artwork by Stephen Alcorn. The poetry will help bring students to a deeper appreciation for people of other places and other times but could also help them form connections to themselves—where they come from, where they've visited, where they would like to go. As students learn more about world cultures, selected poems could be used in making comparisons with people in other countries. Since the poems are organized according to region, groups of students could focus on a different region and pull together other resources and texts to expand their knowledge of that area of the country, then report on it to the whole group. But this is a collection that is beautiful as it stands—to read and savor along with the informational text used in social studies programs.

Heartland, written by Diane Siebert celebrates the Midwest, a region of the U.S. known for its farmland and vast fields of corn and wheat. The narrative verse in this text, as evidenced in the sample lines below, is a fitting tribute to the life of a farmer and the land he works.

from HEARTLAND

The farmer, with his spirit strong;
The farmer, working hard and long,
A feed-and-seed-store cap in place,
Pulled down to shield a weathered face—
A face whose every crease and line
Can tell a tale, and help define
A lifetime spent beneath the sun,
A life of work that's never done.

The verse in this book is simple and straightforward, and the paintings by Wendell Minor are lovely companions to this acknowledgement of a vanishing way of life.

Perhaps no single individual exemplifies hard work, honesty, and determination more than the cowboy. Truly an American icon, the cowboy and his life on the wide-open range is a fascinating topic for study. To celebrate the life of the cowboy, Paul B. Janeczko compiled a wonderful collection of poems for an anthology titled *Home on the Range: Cowboy Poetry*. From ranching, cattle drives, branding and rodeos, to a cowboy's sense of fairness and justice, to the unique gear of the cowboy—his boots, Stetson, saddle, spurs, chaps—the poems allow us to revel in a nostalgic look at the history of cowboys. The following poem by Red Steagall suggests that the era of the cowboy is not yet over.

HATS OFF TO THE COWBOY

The city folks think that it's over.
The cowboy has outlived his time—
An old worn-out relic, a thing of the past,
But the truth is, he's still in his prime.

The cowboy's the image of freedom,
The hard-ridin' boss of the range.
His trade is a fair one, he fights for what's right,
And his ethics aren't subject to change.

He still tips his hat to the ladies,
Let's you water first at the pond.
He believes a day's pay is worth a day's work,
And his handshake and word are his bond.

Bring in a CD of cowboy songs to play when you share the poems from this collection, and alternate cowboy poetry with cowboy songs for a fitting tribute to the cowboy way of life. Once you set the stage with poetry and music, students are eager to engage in other activities involving the study of cowboys. One extension activity that works well with all age levels is to bring in related books about cowboys and the concept of "open range," including information about brands—what they looked like, what they meant, and why they were necessary in the Wild West. As a culmination of their research and reporting about brands, students can design and name their own brand to identify themselves or their family. Additionally, an activity in which students compare and contrast the cowboy with his urban counterpart promotes higher-level thinking and often results in some fairly provocative discussions of justice, ethics, character, and the like.

An anthology compiled by Naomi Shihab Nye, *This Same Sky: A Collection of Poems from Around the World*, features poets from 68 countries, none of whom were born in the U.S. These poems ask us to extend our borders and to broaden our outlook to see not only the differences but also the similarities with our brothers and sisters around the world. The Chilean poet Pablo Neruda wrote this one:

WHAT IS IT THAT UPSETS VOLCANOES

What is it that upsets the volcanoes
that spit fire, cold and rage?

Why wasn't Christopher Columbus
able to discover Spain?

How many questions does a cat have?

Do tears not yet spilled
wait in small lakes?

Or are they invisible rivers
that run toward sadness?

Poetry's connection to the wide array of topics in social studies curriculum is much like that in science—virtually limitless. If it's a topic involving people—cultures, customs, countries, the entire *history* of people and their places—it's available to us in poetry. Take any good anthology and check it out. Page through any collection or volume of poetry that has poems about people and try not to think of connections to social studies. It can hardly be done!

POETRY AND LANGUAGE ARTS

This entire chapter is devoted to advancing the idea of giving poetry a place in every area of the curriculum. Sadly, it is often missing from the one area where it would seem to make the most sense—reading and language arts. Since words and language and the love and power of language form the very essence of poetry, its pairing with language arts and reading is as natural a combination as a kid and a puddle. Bring one to the other, and there's no stopping the impulse to splash around and have fun. Exploring this intrinsic connection could easily take an entire book, or even several volumes, and still there would be more to say about the possibilities. So I will mention a mere handful of suggestions for including poetry in the language arts program, ways that specifically address literacy standards related to reading, writing, speaking, and listening. At the same time, these activities involving poetry are like bringing "the puddle" to the learning process. It's hard to resist.

Point of View

Poetry can be helpful in teaching students to identify point of view, especially since most poems have a perspective that is revealed through implicit rather than explicit cues. At times, however, the "speaker" is more obvious and the reader's task is simply to imagine who is saying the poem or having the thoughts within it. Such is the case with *Prayers from the Ark & the Creatures' Choir*, a collection of poems written by French poet Carmen Bernos de Gasztold and translated into English by novelist Rumer Godden. Translations from one language into another are difficult, none perhaps more so than translating French into English. Likewise, given the brevity of most poems, the accurate translation of each word and each turn of phrase becomes that much more essential in retaining the tone, meaning, and beauty of the poem. Before sharing poems from this collection, discuss the importance and difficulty of the translation process with students to heighten their appreciation for the result. Here is one example from the book written from an animal's point of view. A word of caution: do be sensitive to your students' beliefs and offer another assignment if you suspect this one might make some uncomfortable.

THE PRAYER OF THE LITTLE DUCKS

Dear God,
give us a flood of water.
Let it rain tomorrow and always.
Give us plenty of little slugs to eat.
Protect all folk who quack
and everyone who knows how to swim.
Amen

Reading this and several other point-of-view prayer poems in my language arts class led to an engaging writing exercise: students selected an animal and then wrote their own version of a prayer poem, taking on that creature's point of view. Before they could attempt to "get into the mind" of that animal, the specific traits, behaviors, and needs of the animal had to be considered. Additionally, we examined "prayer language"—the use of particular words characteristic of prayers such as *grant, bestow, protect, deliver, humble,* and *beseech.* We regularly do this same kind of vocabulary exercise with other genres; for example, we draw attention to familiar story language in fairy tales such as *once upon a time, long ago,* and *happily ever after.* Each genre or example within genres gives us this opportunity for exploring language and the distinct vocabulary used within it. The following is one student's prayer written from the point of view of a dog:

THE LITTLE DOG'S PRAYER

Dear God,
Please let tomorrow
be splendid for my walk,
and please no cats!
Have my master be kind
and treat me like royalty.
Provide wieners and bacon
plus many, many shoes to chew.
Amen

This writing activity allowed students a chance to explore a type of writing stance, or purpose, that was unusual yet highly effective. They used thesauruses to support the use of unfamiliar or uncommon vocabulary words and also enjoyed taking on the persona of a creature unlike themselves for a change. It also made them eager to hear more of the poetry from the collection.

Fables Told in Verse

While most students have some familiarity with fables as a literary type, few have encountered them written in verse. Jane Yolen (1995) has written *A Sip of Aesop* in just that way. Yolen's rhymed account of each story is skillful, concise, and captivating. Here are a couple of rhymed morals that capture the "lesson" to be learned, often with a play on words. See if you can guess which fables they're from.

> *High or low upon the vine,*
> *Sour grapes make an awful whine.*

> *Cry wolf once, you'll be believed.*
> *Cry wolf lots, And you'll be grieved.*

This collection is a unique companion to the more traditional prose versions of Aesop's fables. It features many examples of figurative language and double entendre sprinkled throughout. As an example of how to summarize the gist of a story, it's ideal.

Connections to Literature

Without question, one of the most popular novels I've used through the years as a read-aloud with intermediate students has been *Roll of Thunder, Hear My Cry* by Mildred Taylor. Set in Mississippi in the 1930s, the story presents in lavish detail the importance of family, the advantages of hard work and education, and the bitter reality and painful consequences of racial prejudice. It is full of triumph and defeat, loyalty and betrayal, agony, pride, cruelty and fear—a poignant story that features the sharp contrast of hope living alongside despair. After we have shared this book together and experienced a range of deep emotion in response to its compelling nature, the story calls us back to it in various ways. From time to time, we make connections to it with other things we read.

One such connection is through the use of poems such as "Incident" by Countee Cullen (see page 14 for the full text of this poem). This poem captures in stark manner the shock of prejudice in a young boy unaccustomed to it. Read the poem and note your own internal reaction to it. When you share it with students, draw attention to the words in the beginning of the poem that convey the lighthearted demeanor of the boy and which stand in sharp contrast to what comes in the middle and at the end. Students are particularly moved by the impact of this poem, which leads naturally to the work of other African-American poets and broadens their understanding of *Roll of Thunder*. The next idea for weaving poetry into a unit of study in language arts can be seen this way.

Integrating Various Genres

One of the most natural ways to include poetry in the curriculum is to make it one of several pieces of literature brought together around a single theme or subject. The idea of an author/poet study is not new, but frequently poetry is the forgotten resource in this type of study. It doesn't need to be that way since poetry about a wide range of topics is so accessible.

In planning a poet study of Langston Hughes, there are many informational and literary resources available to draw from, and in this case poetry texts seem to dominate the field. To begin this study, I use *Coming Home, from the Life of Langston Hughes* (Floyd Cooper, 1994). This beautifully illustrated biographical account of Hughes's early life provides some understanding of the poet as a young boy, his loneliness and sense of displacement, and his yearning to find a place to belong and feel at home. We learn from this book that his poetry was at least partly a result of this deep longing and loneliness. The book also sets the stage for a closer look at various poems from *The Dream Keeper and Other Poems*, a book of Hughes's poetry. Because students have already learned something of his background in *Coming Home*, Hughes's poems resonate more deeply. See Chapter 6 for an in-depth look at of a discussion of his poetry.

Another book to use is *Love to Langston* (2002), a biographical account of Hughes's life told in verse by poet Tony Medina. Once again, we read about Hughes's lonely childhood, his poverty, and his eventual success as a writer of the Harlem Renaissance. One particularly powerful poem in this collection, "I Do Not Like My Father Much," deals with Hughes's estrangement from his father and reveals much about their relationship. Here are the beginning lines of the poem:

> *I do not like my father much*
> *he is selfish and angry and*
> *calls black people such-and-such*
>
> *I do not like what he has to say*
> *that writing poems for a living*
> *will not pay*

The engaging illustrations by R. Gregory Christie combine with Medina's innovative poetry to celebrate the life of one of the most notable African-American poets ever. As an added feature, Medina has included several pages of biographical notes at the back of the book to provide a larger context for each of the poems. Essentially, we're getting two books in one—poetry in the front and throughout and informational text in the back.

One more book to include is *Visiting Langston*, written by Willie Perdomo and illustrated by Bryan Collier (2002). This book is told in simple verse from the point of view of a young girl going with her father to visit the famous poet's house in Harlem. She feels an affinity for the poet because she, too, is from "Harlem world" and loves to write poetry "just like Langston Hughes." The author's note at the beginning of the book gives information about the poet that is similar to what the other books said:

> He said he wrote most of his poetry when he was sad and, judging by all the poems he wrote, he must have been sad a lot of the time. I think what made him sad was how people, especially people of color, were treated.

Oftentimes, this type of anecdotal information is a springboard for lively discussion about a person's work—how one's situation in life, experiences, and family relationships provide a framework for writing.

Biographical Poems

To continue this biographical theme, one more book deserves mention. Ann Whitford Paul (1999) wrote *All by Herself*, a collection of poetry written about women, some famous, some not so well known, including Amelia Earhart, Wilma Rudolph, Pocahontas, and Wanda Gag. The lines below are from the end of the poem about Sacajawea, another woman included in this collection:

> *So many hills to climb . . .*
> *traveling on for two years' time,*
> *trudging, tramping day by day,*
> *wending, winding on her way,*
> *with every dauntless step she took,*
> *she walked into our history books.*

Each of these 14 biographical poems is a tribute to the personal courage, daring, and determination of a young woman at some point in history. Some you will easily recognize, others not, but all are inspiring stories told in verse. Added to informational texts and picture books about these women, or others like them, *All by Herself* can be used as a resource for writing character sketches or drawing comparisons between women. The style of these poems could also serve as a model for students in writing biographical summaries of other individuals—in verse instead of the traditional prose.

Perplexed by Spelling Patterns?

Let's face it—one area of many language arts programs that gets short shrift is spelling. But one way to liven things up and have some fun with it is by offering a poem now and then that features some of the frustrating aspects of spelling patterns of the English language. This one by Eve Merriam illustrates that even rules we thought we could count on don't always stand the test.

> ### WHY I DID NOT REIGN
>
> *I longed to win the spelling bee*
> *And remembered the rule*
> *I had learned in school:*
>
> *"I before E,*
> *Except after C."*
>
> *Friend, believe me,*
> *No one was going to deceive me.*

Fiercely I practiced, the scepter I'd wield,
All others their shields in the field would yield!

Alas, before my very eyes
A weird neighbor in a beige veil
Feigning great height and weighty size
Seized the reins and ran off with the prize.

Now I no longer deign to remember that rule.
Neither
Any other either.

When trying to offer students help in learning spelling patterns, we also try to teach them exceptions to the rules. But, alas, as this poem points out, sometimes the number of exceptions makes the rule almost impossible to follow. Would you call that "unwieldy"?!

For another clever look at spelling patterns—this time the "ough" pattern—read Alice Schertle's "Consider Cow," which starts like this:

Consider cow
which rhymes
with bough
but not
with rough.
That's clear
enough.

It's hard for anyone to resist this lighthearted approach to an often dry aspect of language arts. Many other poems offer a similarly bright perspective on our complicated language.

THE GOLDEN THREAD OF POETRY

Weaving poetry into the curriculum can be the single most dramatic and effective way to vitalize your classroom and is within every teacher's capability. As you weave it in and out, day by day, poetry can be the golden thread that makes the fabric of your classroom environment luminous. Along the way, students discover the joy of poetry, the exquisite magic of it, an appreciation that may last for years. "For when you throw a stone into the water, it's hard to tell how far the ripples go." And while poetry may not be the heart of your curriculum, it may very well be its soul.

In this chapter we've seen the way poetry connects to content-area subjects. The next chapter takes a look at the dynamic way poetry can be used to make meaningful connections to students' lives.

CHAPTER SIX

Using Poetry to Connect to Students' Lives:

Powerful Ways to Engage and Motivate Students with Poetry

> *People think they can do without poetry. And they can. At least until they fall in love, lose a friend, lose a child, or a parent, or lose their way in the dark woods of life. People think they can live without poetry. And they can. At least until they become fatally ill, have a baby, or fall desperately, madly, in love.*
>
> ~ Erica Jong

In previous chapters, poetry was seen as a genre to be explored and celebrated, a means of introducing poetic and literary elements, a stimulus for written response or discussion, an inspiration for creative extension activities, and an integral component of content-area subjects. This chapter will highlight what is possibly poetry's finest feature—its ability to connect to the minds and hearts of its listeners. In the words of one of my female students: "Poetry makes me feel like I belong somewhere." If that were all poetry ever did, it would be enough, but there's so much more poetry can do for us and our students. Let's take a look.

FINDING THE WORDS WE NEED

The world is an amazing yet complicated place, and it can be difficult at times to find our place in it. This is especially true for middle school students, who are just beginning to develop their sense of self and discover how they fit into the larger world. They are in flux, experiencing rapid physical growth, negotiating increasingly complex relationships, moving from concrete to abstract thinking. All these changes are unsettling, and I've found that poetry often expresses the intense emotions students are feeling. According to Georgia Heard (1999), "we read poetry from this deep hunger to know ourselves and the world." Poetry offers students a way to satisfy this hunger and to better understand themselves and others. As one of my students said, "Poetry makes me feel really open, and it can touch your heart."

Poetry Helps Us Understand Ourselves

The function of poets, wrote Wallace Stevens (in Andrews, 1991), is to "help people live their lives." No matter how commonplace an event or emotion might be, a poet can shape it into something meaningful, something valuable. For poet William Stafford, a feeling of simple happiness became this poem:

ANY MORNING

Just lying on the couch and being happy.
Only humming a little, the quiet sound in the head.
Trouble is busy elsewhere at the moment, it has
so much to do in the world.

People who might judge are mostly asleep; they can't
monitor you all the time, and sometimes they forget.
When dawn flows over the hedge you can
get up and act busy.

Little corners like this, pieces of Heaven
left lying around, can be picked up and saved.
People won't even see that you have them,
they are so light and easy to hide.

Later in the day you can act like the others.
You can shake your head. You can frown.

In the hands of a poet such as Stafford, an ordinary moment is captured and transformed into something remarkable and even poignant. Reading poetry like this helps students value their everyday experiences, reflect on them, and explore what is truly meaningful in their lives. After reading "Any Morning" to a class, I encourage students to offer examples of simple contentment or joy from their own experience. They mention things like *receiving a good grade, the loyalty of a friend, wearing a new shirt*, and *a cute guy (or girl) smiling at you*. I help them see that any of these examples could be material for a poem.

Having personally experienced the way poetry so often enriches normal activities, I want to revisit that experience again and again. I see myself in poems. I know more about my own heart through these poems. As a teacher, I want to bring this experience to my students to help them learn more about themselves. I do this on a regular basis by sharing poems that are personally meaningful to me, such as this one by Emily Dickinson:

IF I CAN STOP ONE HEART FROM BREAKING

If I can stop one heart from breaking,
I shall not live in vain;
If I can ease one life the aching,
Or cool one pain,

Or help one fainting robin
Unto his next again,
I shall not live in vain.

After reading it aloud, I tell students, "This poem captures an ideal vision of what I'd like my life to be about: helping others, being compassionate, caring about another's pain. I fall short much of the time, but Dickinson's words give me something to strive for. It reminds me of the person I want to be." This kind of sharing helps reveal the person I am inside (and may not always show on the outside) and also the way a poem can express what's in the deepest part of us. By modeling this personal connection, I help students become more comfortable with allowing poetry to speak to them in similar ways.

I want students to feel for themselves the helpful and, at times, even healing, power of words. With that in mind, I need to be sensitive to and watchful for openings that arise out of need or circumstance. I often choose specific poems to share with students that acknowledge the difficult realities we all face—hurt feelings, confusion, friendship or relationship problems, the death or illness of a parent or grandparent, and other personal concerns. When I share poems, for example, from *Been to Yesterdays: Poems of a Life* by Lee Bennett Hopkins, students who have experienced divorce in the family knowingly nod their heads with understanding at these words from the book:

ANOTHER

long
drawn-out
night

another
bitter, brutal
fight.

Time
stood still
till
morning
broke
with a
trembling
throbbing
terrored-force—

as
I woke up
sleepily
half-believing
I hadn't
heard
the
dreaded
word—

divorce.

Divorce is a sensitive and often excruciatingly painful subject for young people to deal with, so not every student will be comfortable commenting openly about the feelings this poem taps into—feelings of loss, anger, fear, abandonment, confusion, or even relief. I don't ever force discussion with poems that tackle such difficult realities, but I often try to open discussion with a question like, "Does anyone have a thought they'd like to share about this poem or this topic?" Usually there's some brave soul willing to offer an opinion or personal memory this poem stirs up, and then other students are more inclined to join in. Sometimes, a written response is an easier and more suitable way for students to express personal connections to difficult topics like this one. Other times, there is such obvious emotion evoked—apparent in the way a student buries her head in her arms, looks stricken, or becomes tearful—that I just let the poem settle quietly in the heart of each individual without asking for or expecting any outward response at all. In this case, I make a brief statement acknowledging the intense emotions such poems can elicit: "There are times a poem reaches right in and grabs our hearts, jolting us with its truth. When that happens, it can be uncomfortable—but it can also help us realize we're not alone in the world, no matter what we're feeling." And that kind of connection, whether to the poet, the poem, or a handful of peers, can be incredibly comforting and reassuring.

By sharing sensitive poetry that deals with difficult issues, we convey the message that we care about our students' lives, both in school and out. It's a way of showing them that we're concerned for their emotions as well as their intellect. Poetry that taps into all aspects of life—the monumental and the mundane—can be a powerful companion in a caring classroom.

Donald Murray (1996) recognizes the importance of sharing the ordinary, commonplace particulars of a life. He says,

> Poetry is not contained in great thoughts, distant visions, but in the materials of our individual lives, the specific, resonating details that will reveal the meaning of our lives and will cause others, when they read of our lives, to discover their own.

This discovery of self may be an awareness we're not even looking for, or don't know we need. Poetry can provide that awareness and fill that need. When we feel a strong connection to a poem, it is often because our own reality has been illuminated. We sigh with relief and our souls sing out with that *"yes! yes!"* of being understood and therefore validated.

Poetry Helps Us Understand Others

At other times we may be amazed or humbled to discover through poetry how others live and think and feel. This experience is powerful for middle school students, who often are caught up in their own lives and have difficulty seeing the perspective of others. Poetry is one avenue to expand their awareness and understanding of other people's points of view. As we see differences as well as similarities, we recognize our own place and also come to appreciate others'. Few of us, for example, will know the challenges of being blind, but this poem by Mary O'Neill, from *Fingers Are Always Bringing Me News* gives us at least partial entry into that world:

MIMI'S FINGERS

I am blind. All that I can see
My enchanted fingers bring to me,
As if all sight were mingled with all touch
I do not mind not-seeing very much.
In Braille I read the words these fingers trace,
And with them come to know your smile, your face,
Your buckled shoes, the silk-thread of your hair,
The fabric of each suit and dress you wear;
All shapes, all sizes, how long, how far, how high,
How round a bowl, how gently curved the sky,
How pointed the far tip-top of a hill,
The narrow table of a window sill.
I know a snowflake as a melting star,
The sticky-thick of honey and of tar.
Color alone my fingers cannot do.
Could you, could you, tell me about blue?

Other poems from this collection are equally adept at bringing students into the world of others, some of whom may be just like them while others not at all. I like sharing poems of this nature because it gives us the chance to talk about the many ways we are alike—our commonalities—as well as the ways we are unique—our diversity. Poet Robert Kendall (in Lockward, 1994) offers his view on the value of sharing poetry with our students.

> Poetry is a means for seeing the world in new ways, for gaining new insights on old
> problems. Learning to read poetry can also help people learn to read the world better.
> It can teach them to look beyond assumptions and prejudices, to look beneath the
> appearance of people or situations, to look past temporary unhappiness or failure.

Through lively and thought-provoking class discussions (see Chapter 3 for details on types of discussion formats) based on poems like "Mimi's Fingers," we are able to make strong connections to others and also to ourselves.

Poetry Can Bring Us Together

"The poet," writes Gregory Denman (1988), "serves as a caretaker of the human experience." We see this to be true in the following poem by Eloise Greenfield:

THIS PLACE

There is this place I know
where children go to find
their deepest feelings
they look behind the trees
for hiding wants and angers
bashful joys
this place is quiet
no shouts may enter

no rolling laughter
but only silent tears
to carry the feelings
forward in waves
that wash the children
whole

In a post-9/11 world, "This Place" offers soothing words for frightening times. I share poems from this book to answer a deep need I see in middle school students. The impact of terrorism, specifically the horrific events of September 11, is a reality we now live with on a daily basis. Young adolescents want and need an outlet for the resulting emotions of that reality. This is evident in the way students frequently bring up ongoing and troubling events, their fear and uncertainty, their almost desperate hope for a safer world. One morning students brought up the war in Iraq and talked about their concerns—*What will happen next? What might Iraq or terrorists do to retaliate? Would loved ones in the military come home safely?* Many expressed grave doubts that this world would ever be secure. This kind of conversation happens regularly. Poetry from *This Place I Know* (selected by Georgia Heard) serves as a wonderful catalyst for discussion at the same time it grounds us and gives us something good to hang onto, like the hope expressed in these closing lines from another poem in the book, "A Little Girl's Poem" by Gwendolyn Brooks: "Life is for us, and is shining. / We have a right to sing." Sharing poetry that speaks of hope and courage and goodness and peace puts us in touch with our deep longing for those things and at the same time brings a measure of comfort to our souls.

The use of poetry to acknowledge events that concern us, whether on a global or national scale or in the smaller sphere of our personal lives, shows sensitivity for the complex emotions we all have, establishes our connection to the human family, and gives us the words our hearts need to say.

MAKING PERSONAL CONNECTIONS THROUGH READING POETRY

Most of the time, it's easy to see the way students relate to a given poem. You can tell from their body language; their pensive, agitated, or excited appearance; the depth of written responses; the lively and often provocative discussions. And I've gotten pretty good at knowing which poems are likely to draw out those reactions. But every now and then, I can still be surprised by the way a poem seems to grip a student in some unexpected way. Here's an example of what I mean.

One morning, a fourth grader named Hannah approached my desk to tell me she'd spent part of the previous evening looking at Emily Dickinson poems and had found one she particularly liked. Hannah asked if she could read it to the class. "Of course," I said, "but could I see the one you chose?" I was a bit unprepared for what she handed me—a copy of the following poem, one of many Dickinson wrote about death:

THE CHARIOT

Because I could not stop for Death,
He kindly stopped for me;
The carriage held but just ourselves
And Immortality.

We slowly drove, he knew no haste,
And I had put away
My labor, and my leisure too,
For his civility.

We passed the school where children played,
Their lessons scarcely done;
We passed the fields of grazing grain,
We passed the setting sun.

We paused before a house that seemed
A swelling of the ground;
The roof was scarcely visible,
The cornice but a mound.

Since then 'tis centuries; but each
Feels shorter than the day
I first surmised the horses' heads
Were toward eternity.

I have to admit, this wasn't characteristic of the more lighthearted, humorous, or contemporary poems students typically choose to share. I was curious about why she selected it and wondered whether she was clear about the poem's theme or even understood it. "What made you choose this poem, Hannah? Did someone you care about die recently?"

"No," she answered. "I liked how serious the poem was and the way the poet wrote about Death as if it was a person."

"Can you tell me more about what you liked in this poem?" I asked.

"Well, it makes you realize that we're all going to die, but death doesn't have to be something you're afraid of," she said. "The poem makes Death sound . . . patient and kind and polite to the person he's coming to get. I just like that."

"So the topic of death doesn't bother you?" I said.

"Not really," Hannah said. "The way the poem is written makes death sound peaceful."

Hannah's self-assurance as she readily answered my questions demonstrated that she clearly understood the poem, and I could see in her earnestness that its theme had deeply touched her in some way. She was eager to share that connection with the rest of us. I was anxious to hear Hannah read the poem to her classmates, and to see their reactions to it.

Before she began, I told the class that her selection was a serious one, a poem that Hannah felt personally drawn to for various reasons, and that we could talk about it when she was done. They settled in to listen. As she walked to the front of the class and prepared to read, I was struck by the way Hannah's demeanor changed from schoolgirl casual to more somber and dignified. Her posture straightened and she stood very still for a few seconds. Then she began to speak in a clear but solemn voice. Her quiet expression as she read and the look of peaceful resignation on her face set the perfect tone for this poem. I had to remind myself this was a 10-year-old reading it! When she'd finished, there was a respectful hush for several moments. And then the conversation took off.

As surprised as I was by Hannah's choice of poems, I was equally impressed with the discussion that followed. The subject of death was taken up without hesitation and with no apparent fear. I can't recall the exact words of our conversation, but I remember that it initially focused on the strong images presented in the poem: the figure of Death—the driver of the "chariot" or "carriage" that came to pick up its intended passenger—and the carriage itself. Students shared their impressions of these images with comments like these:

> "The poem says 'He kindly stopped for me' so Death is a man. I think he's dressed in black, and looks like a gentleman."

> "I think he had on a tall black hat and suit, and wore white gloves."

> "I see a tall man, dressed up in fancy black clothes, who was very quiet on their trip to eternity."

> "The carriage is shiny and black and is being pulled by two black horses. It looks very expensive."

> "In my mind, the carriage is the kind a queen or other royalty would ride in. It's black and has red velvet seats."

The discussion also involved the passenger—perhaps the poet?—who garnered her fair share of comments, and went something like this:

> "It sounds like the person Death came for was either too busy or didn't want to stop living yet."

> "But when Death came for her, she had no choice except to get in the carriage."

> "It didn't sound like she put up any fight about it, though. She got in as if she realized it had to happen sooner or later."

> "As they were on their trip to heaven, or wherever eternity is, they passed by ordinary places that used to be part of her life–a school, some fields, a house. It was like she knew she was seeing them for the last time."

"Yeah, but she didn't seem upset. Maybe sort of sad that her life in the world was really over. I'll probably feel the same way when I die."

The conversation went on this way for some 15 to 20 minutes, and all the while I felt gratified by this improbable turn of events. I could never have guessed that this particular poem would be at all meaningful to such a young audience. But because of Hannah's personal connection, an unlikely poem had given rise to a rich and satisfying experience for all of us. Such an event highlights the wisdom in letting go of preconceived notions regarding the kinds of poems kids will like and appreciate. It reminds me to give personal preferences a place in poetry sharing.

MAKING PERSONAL CONNECTIONS THROUGH WRITING POETRY

So often in life, something happens that tugs at the heart in such a compelling way that it almost demands some type of response to signify it. For some, simply talking about it with another is enough. A few may want to write in a diary. Others may decide to keep their thoughts and emotions held inside. And then there are times when nothing else will do but to capture the experience and our feelings about it in a poem. Isn't this, in fact, what inspires most poetry? I almost take this for granted when reading poetry written by "professional" poets. Most students, however, don't typically think of writing poetry as a way to express themselves. I try to foster this kind of response to something we've read or experienced by gently encouraging them to share their thoughts and feelings in a poem. To model such a personal response, we sometimes write a free verse poem together as a group, which might lead them to dabble in it on their own. When a student does choose to express herself in a poem, a distinct current of excitement runs through me, especially when the result is as impressive as the one written by a former student of mine. Let me tell you about it.

Alison was a bright, talented young girl with a ready smile and a great sense of humor. She was also highly sensitive, so it was not surprising that she would be strongly affected when I read aloud excerpts from the book *Nightjohn* (Gary Paulsen, 1993), a historically accurate account of the stark realities of slavery. We all found the story of Sarny, a slave girl, and Nightjohn, an older slave who secretly taught other slaves to read and write, riveting in its details yet difficult to hear. Alison was so deeply touched that she had to put her feelings into words—words that found their way into the following poem (originally published in Perfect, 1999):

LONG AGO

Long ago
there were
slaves.
Their masters
acting strong
holding that
long
whip
that hit

their hard
working
backs with red
thick
blood
running down.

Masters thinking
slaves are just
       nothing but
dogs that are
to work
in the fields
and eat out of a
trough
       like pigs.

When she handed me her poem to read, I was literally stunned speechless. Here was a 9-year-old, no bigger than a minute, with a poem so immense and so heavy in its impact, it almost takes my breath away to remember it. At the time, Alison could see from the tears in my eyes the profound effect her poem had on me. As we looked at each other, there was no need for words between us. All I could say was, "Oh, Alison…" We felt a deep connection to each other, to her poem, and to the book *Nightjohn*.

Alison's response to a poignant story inspired her to write "Long Ago," a poem both eloquent and horrible in its insight. It was one instance in which a deep personal connection *with* a poem and *to* a poem became an experience we'd both remember for a long time.

CONNECTING TO THE POETRY OF LANGSTON HUGHES

Poetry has the power to speak to students about issues important to them in a way no other genre can. As we've seen in previous sections, poetry can form a bridge to students, giving us a way to connect to them personally. We can make that connection deeper by delving into poems that engage students and by exploring those poems fully. This process builds their understanding of poetic elements in a meaningful way. This next lesson on the poetry of Langston Hughes shows how a fortuitous poetry sharing led to one of those remarkable discussions.

Reading and Responding to "Reasons Why"

One morning, I grabbed a collection of Langston Hughes poetry from my shelf to get our day going. I told my students a little about the poet, that he was African American, was born in 1902 and died in 1967, and that he lived for a time in nearby Cleveland, Ohio. Though previous classes had enjoyed it, this was the first time I'd shared any of the poetry from *The Dream Keeper and Other Poems* with this current group of fourth graders. Randomly, I selected the poem "Reasons Why" (a short love poem written in dialect) and read it to the class. The poem ends with these two lines:

> *Ma heart's a fluttering aspen leaf*
> *When you pass by.*

I asked my students to notice that the poet says his heart is something else, reminding them to look for the shared quality or characteristic between two things. Looking at a sea of blank faces, I sensed a little help was in order. I explained that an aspen tree has leaves that quiver, or "flutter," on their stems with even the slightest breeze; the quivering aspen leaf was being compared to a heart in love. Some lights of recognition went on and smiles crossed the students' faces. This was a group that was highly sensitive to boy/girl interests and attachments, however fleeting. This, by golly, was a poem they could relate to! Here are some of their responses:

"Well, when a person you love walks by, your heart starts pounding faster."

"I laugh a lot."

"I get nervous when someone I like comes around me. I start sweating and my jaw drops."

"My heart pumps a little faster."

"Sometimes I don't know what to say—I just stare at them."

A brief explanation of the aspen tree was all this group needed to spark response and discussion. Once they understood the "behavior" of an aspen leaf, the image of the poet's metaphor became clear. This is the type of scaffolding, the support we give "at the edge of a child's competence" (Gaskins et al., 1997), that makes all the difference between surface and down-to-the-bone understanding. The success students had with the imagery in this poem enabled them to form a personally meaningful response to it and enjoy it on a deeper level. At the same time, it increased their confidence as well as the likelihood they would grasp figurative language in other poetry. It also made them eager for more.

Reading and Responding to "Mother to Son"

Reading and responding to "Reasons Why" had taken barely five minutes. It had been a brief but engaging experience so I decided to try another. I paged through *The Dream Keeper* until I came to one of Langston Hughes's most familiar poems, "Mother to Son." Before reading, I asked students to listen to the voice doing the talking in the poem, to imagine who it was and what we might know about her from her words. The room grew quiet as I began:

MOTHER TO SON

Well, son, I'll tell you:
Life for me ain't been no crystal stair.
It's had tacks in it,
And splinters,
And boards torn up,
And places with no carpet on the floor—
Bare.
But all the time
I'se been a-climbin' on,
And reachin' landin's,

And turnin' corners,
And sometimes goin' in the dark
Where there ain't been no light.
So, boy, don't you turn back.
Don't you set down on the steps
'Cause you finds it kinder hard.
Don't you fall now—
For I'se still goin', honey,
I'se still climbin',
And life for me ain't been no crystal stair.

When I finished reading, I waited a few moments to give the poem and its words time to settle in. Then I asked: "What did you notice? What are you thinking?" Several hands went up to comment on the person speaking in the poem:

"The title of the poem is 'Mother to Son' so we already know a mother is the one talking."

"It seems like she has a lot of trouble."

"It sounds like she's been through a lot."

"I think the mother is African American by the way she talks, and because an African American wrote the poem."

"Some of the words she says, her accent—she doesn't have a high vocabulary, so maybe she can't read. She's not very well educated."

I wanted to read the poem again to see what more we could get from it. "This time," I said, "let's listen to what the poet says the mother's life has been like and the comparison he makes. Picture the image Langston Hughes is giving us."

After this second reading, our conversation focused on the image of the "crystal stair" and what the mother's life had been like. We noticed that the poet told us right away that her life had *not* been a crystal stair and then described the way it had been instead—with tacks, splinters, and torn-up boards. This contrast seemed to be at the heart of the image, so I asked them what a "crystal stair" would be like to them. Here are some of their responses:

HANNAH: "It would be smooth and gentle on your feet."

SAMANTHA: "It would be pleasant because you're walking up a smooth thing."

JESSICA: "It would be easy to go up. There would be no boards torn up like the mother said, so it wouldn't be as hard to climb up."

RYAN: "If you were walking on it in your bare feet, it would be cool."

MEGAN: "I just think of it as smooth."

SAMANTHA: "Yeah, it would be like ice—it would be smooth and you would glide on it."

JESSICA: "It would feel better than the kind she's mentioned."

JENNA: "I think of how crystal forms rainbows on the wall when light goes through it and how pretty that is."

I asked them to consider why the poet chose this particular word, *crystal*, to form his image. I said, "I've never seen a crystal stair, and I'm a lot older than you are, so to me the image is an unusual one. What do you think about it?" Posing such questions about word choice (also rhyme scheme, line breaks, etc.) helps students begin to realize what the craft of poetry involves. Of all the words or images Hughes could have used, these were the ones he chose. These choices are not random; they are carefully thought-out decisions. The discussion about the word *crystal* continued with these ideas:

NATHAN: "Maybe it's the first word he thought of."

JESSICA: "Maybe he was thinking of how it is sparkling and smooth."

MEGAN: "Crystal is expensive so it's worth a lot."

REBECCA: "Maybe he just liked the word and how it sounded."

LINDSEY: "Or maybe he liked how it sounded with the other words in the poem."

Lindsey's comment seemed like a good place to draw attention to the *st* sound repeated in the words *crystal stair* as an example of alliteration. "Maybe Langston Hughes decided he wanted exactly these two words because he liked how they sounded together, as Lindsey suggested," I said.

Then I posed this question: "What else might have worked in the poem?" Nathan thought the poet could've used *glass stair* or *silver stair* because the *s* sound goes with *stair*. Hannah said that *marble* might also work. Samantha suggested *gold* "because it's rich, though it doesn't really go with *stair*." Ryan added that *golden stair* sounded better than just *gold*. We agreed on the merits of these words, that we could "see" these images, too, and that they shared some of the qualities of crystal: smooth, hard, worth a lot. I said that although there is no way of knowing for sure what the poet's intention was, it's fun to speculate on the choices he made since word choice, imagery, and other elements of poetry add so much to meaning and are carefully conceived to leave just the right impression on the reader. I reminded students of the comparison between prose and poetry that I'd shared in an earlier lesson: prose is the use of words in the best order, but poetry uses the *best* words in the *best* order.

"I believe Langston Hughes's use of the word *crystal* was no accident," I continued, "but a deliberate choice. Why this word, not that? Poets choose a word for its meaning, the sound of it, and how it feels on our tongue, and what we picture when we read it." This last comment directed our discussion away from word choice back to the imagery in "Mother to Son"—its most important aspect.

Extending the Discussion: What About Those Stairs?

"The mother is talking to her son about the kind of life she's had," I said. "For her, it's been so different from all those things you said about crystal—pretty, smooth, easy to glide across. How does she describe her life?"

One girl said, "She talks about the kind of stairs she's had to go up, and how hard it was. We have to go up to the third floor every day, carrying heavy bookbags, and your legs really get tired." Someone else added, "There's too many stairs. We need an elevator!" Lots of heads nodded in agreement with this assessment. Since our classroom is on the third floor of the school, we could all relate to the difficulty of going up and down three flights of stairs. Going almost anywhere in the building—the office, the restrooms, the cafeteria, the playground—requires us to make the trip down and back up again. It can be very tiring to do this numerous times every school day.

"Well, we know what our stairs are like," I said. "What does the mother tell us about hers?" The poem's description is explicit, very visual and concrete. Students zeroed in on the words used to tell about what made it hard:

"The poem says her stairs have tacks and splinters in it."

"And it says there are boards torn up, which could be dangerous."

"There's tacks and nails—or whatever—so it feels like forever just trying to climb."

"Ouch!"

"It says there's no carpet on it."

At this last comment, I showed them the text of the poem. "Langston Hughes wrote: 'And places with no carpet on the floor' on one line," I explained, "and the word *bare* by itself on the next. Why do you think he did this?" "I think he did that to make us notice it a lot," one student said. "To draw our attention to it," said another.

"I think you're exactly right," I said. "We really notice a word that's all by itself. Maybe he wanted it to look the same as what the word means—'with nothing around it.' That's what *bare* means, to have nothing on it at all. Her stairs had nothing soft like carpeting to cushion her feet."

"That would be hard," a student added. "It would not be a nice place to walk on."

Sensing our discussion was getting too literal, I wanted to move us back to the poem's figurative meaning: "The poem says the stairs had 'tacks, splinters, and broken boards' on them, but let's remember that the stairs are an image, a symbol for the mother's life. What do these things really mean?"

Nathan said they might mean injuries, or illness and disease. Hannah said, "Life's not always smooth. The tacks may mean obstacles."

"What are obstacles?" I asked.

"Something like a wall—you have to get past it," Hannah added.

"I think an obstacle is something you have to accomplish," Chris said.

Sam thought it could mean having money problems, "like it's hard to pay taxes."

Jesse had this idea of an obstacle: "In life, you have really big choices to make. If you make the wrong choice, you can really mess up your life."

The quality of their responses removed any uncertainty I may have had about whether these children understood symbolism. They were more than adequate; they were articulate. Next, we shifted our focus to the other person implied in the poem—the son receiving his mother's advice and encouragement.

Rereading the last part of the poem, I reminded them that the mother is speaking to her son. "Why is she saying all this to him, do you think?" Their responses demonstrate their comprehension:

> "Maybe he's going through a hard time. She's telling him not to give up because she hasn't, and it hasn't been easy for her."

> "She says that she's still climbing even though it's been hard and that he should, too."

> "She wants him to keep trying."

"Life is like. . ."

Samples of students' original similes:

"Life is like a math test with a bad grade when nobody wants you."

~ *Courtney E.*

"Life could feel like a storm because sometimes it's dark and lonely."

~ *Emma D.*

"Life can feel like a pencil because you're always getting worn down."

~ *Joey H.*

"Life could be like riding a unicycle because it's hard to balance it. Sometimes it's hard to stay equal with other people."

~ *Ty W.*

"Life is like a Rubik's Cube—hard to get it together and make it fit. It can be frustrating and confusing."

~ *Rebecca S.*

"Life is like a book with many chapters to it. It contains bits of everything: joy, sadness, anger, darkness, and mystery."

~ *Samantha L.*

"Life is like a math problem that no one can figure out. Like a confusing math problem, life can be puzzling, frustrating, and difficult."

~ *Lindsey W.*

"Life is like a desert because it's hard to get through."

~ *Brandon S.*

"Life is like a whirlpool—it is very fast and frightening."

~ *Noah M.*

Connecting to Our Own Lives

Though this discussion was already rich and complete and surprising in its depth, I asked one more question. It seemed a perfect time to invite students' own ideas about life to see what image or symbol they would choose to describe it. "The poet wrote this poem about a woman's difficult life," I said. "He chose some stairs to compare it to that had the same qualities as her hard life—broken up, obstacles in her path, hard and dark. Could you think of some other image to use that would represent a hard life?"

After a bit of silence, Nathan's hand went up. "Life can make you feel like you're an ant—very small—and people might not notice you too much. And it's a lot of hard work." His response inspired others to give it a try.

"Life can be like walking a tightrope, when you feel like you could lose your balance and fall," said Jessica.

Tom remembered something about a character from the book *Belle Prater's Boy* (Ruth White, 1996) when he said, "Life is a straitjacket when you feel trapped and can't move. That's how Belle Prater felt before she disappeared."

Briefly, I explained how to create a simile (e.g., "Life is like. . .") and told them that's what they were doing, the same way poets often do. "First, you think of the thing you're trying to represent and the particular qualities you want to highlight. Then think of an unlike object that also has those qualities. That becomes a symbol for the first thing." I offered an example of my own to go along with the few already given. I liked the way Tom made a connection to other literature, so I did the same. "Remember Arnold Adoff's poem in *Love Letters* about the mom, and the way her image was made of puzzle pieces? Well, I'm a mom, so I know how that feels sometimes. My life is like a puzzle—some of my pieces are missing so I'm not all put together. I'm also like a puzzle because I can be hard to figure out. What's your life like at times?"

A healthy sprinkling of hands went up. The kids were really warming to this idea of comparing life to something else.

"Life is like a roller coaster because it has lots of ups and downs."

"Life is like a hurricane when I get mad. I blow up and I'm dangerous."

"Life can be like a fan—you're just going around in circles."

By this time, almost every student had a response they wanted to share. I was amazed and gratified that their examples showed so much insight. Grabbing the teachable moment that had come our way, I asked the class if they wanted to write down their ideas, type them on the computer, and create a bulletin board in the hallway so others could see them. I was proud of their thinking and wanted to showcase their talent for creating metaphors and similes. They, too, were eager to display their work. They had begun to feel the satisfaction of thinking like a poet.

Where Poetry Takes Us

What started as just another poem shared on just another day ended up being so much more. Together we came into the presence of some fairly sophisticated poetry that we not only understood, but also brought to life through sustained, multilayered, and spontaneous discussion. There had been no plan, no structure, no predetermined goal set ahead of time. We let the poetry itself guide us. A brief encounter with one poem, "Reasons Why," led to a more involved and deeper response to another, "Mother to Son."

Of course, not all poetry ends in such a rich and fulfilling experience. But every poem leaves its mark. And I believe the effect of daily or frequent sharing of poetry is cumulative. When poetry is not just an occasional event but an essential piece of the fabric of classroom life, it becomes as natural as breathing in and breathing out. Over time and with many encounters, poetry seeps into the soul and transforms it. Poet Julia Cunningham (in Janeczko, 1990) urges us to "walk with your words into these secret, mysterious, and magic places where poems lead you." Poetry takes us on its own journey. Many times, because of the strong connection a poem makes to our own lives, we are led back to our own selves—a place both mysterious and familiar.

Some Final Thoughts

> It is poetry that changes everything.
>
> ~ bell hooks (in "Black Is a Woman's Color," 1989)

In the process of writing this book, I attempted to stay in touch with friends, partly for balance, partly for sanity, sometimes for serious reality checks. Communication with a friend living on the West Coast was spotty, but occasional e-mails kept us connected. In one of my messages, I told her I was writing a book on poetry for teachers and teacher educators in hopes of encouraging them to include more poetry, more often, in their instruction. Her response just about took my breath away.

Kathy—

Your book on poetry sounds great. I have always loved poems starting with good old Christopher Robin—"When I was one, I had just begun." In high school I had a poetry class and discovered the classical poets like Shelley, Poe, Keats, Coleridge: "Weave a circle around him thrice, and close your eyes in Holy dread, for he on honeydew hath fed, and drunk the milk of paradise." Then I went on to the dark Hermann Hesse: "so I can recover from this life's emptiness and go home to my own dreams." In college it was the feminists like Marge Piercy— "I am tired of finding my enemy in my bed!" and Brautigan's The Pill Versus the Springhill Mine Disaster *and other fun stuff. Life would be so much poorer without poetry.*

Oh, my goodness, yes! I thought. *Life is so much poorer without poetry.* My wish is that all children would grow up knowing and loving poetry so well, like my friend Patty did, so that it stays with them, in one form or another—committed to memory, written in notebooks, collected in volumes—throughout their lives. As teachers, we have a lot of influence on making that happen. That's been my aim with this book—to celebrate poetry and persuade you to give it a place in your classroom and the lives of your students. It is truly in the presence of poetry that so many good things happen.

Glossary

accent emphasis on a syllable; a regularly recurring stress or emphasis in a line of poetry (see *stress*)

aesthetic stance a focus on what happens *during* a reading event, that is, attention on private aspects of meaning such as personal associations, feelings, and ideas being evoked or lived through during the reading

alliteration the repetition of consonant or vowel sounds at the beginning or in the middle of successive words (see *assonance* and *consonance*)

assonance when the vowels in words are the same but the consonants are not.
Ex: *beat/week, gave/tame, light/mine*

ballad a short narrative poem traditionally sung and passed from one generation to another in oral form; written in a four-line stanza with the rhyme scheme *abcb*

blank verse unrhymed verse

cadence often used as a synonym for *rhythm*

cinquain a five-line stanza with two, four, six, eight, and two syllables respectively

concrete poetry poems shaped like the specific object they describe

consonance when the consonants in words are the same but the vowels are not.
Ex: *"maggie and milly and molly and may"* (title of a poem by e.e. cummings)

couplet a stanza of two lines that rhyme and form a unit

efferent stance a focus on what is to be retained *after* the reading act such as facts and information that may later be recalled, analyzed, and so on; attention is on public aspects of meaning

end rhyme rhyme occurring at the end of two or more lines

epic a long narrative poem usually about a hero and his heroic companions; the hero often possesses superhuman and/or divine characteristics

figurative language figures of speech (called *tropes*); the use of literary devices such as simile, metaphor, personification, idioms and so on

foot a group of stressed and unstressed syllables combining to form a unit of verse; a rhythmic unit in a line of poetry

free verse poetry that makes use of natural cadences rather than a fixed metrical pattern; the rhythmical lines vary in length and are usually unrhymed; though it may appear unrestrained, there is a firm pattern to the words

genre a type or category of imaginative literature that is classified according to form, technique, or content (poetry, the novel, short story, essay, etc.); also, types within a kind of literature (the narrative poem, the lyric poem, the ballad, epic, etc.)

haiku a Japanese poem form made up of 17 syllables divided into three lines; generally, the first line has five syllables; the second has seven; the third has five
Ex: *Broken and broken*
 Again on the sea, the moon
 So easily mends
(written by Chosu; translated by Harry Behn)

imagery the use of sensory details or images that appeal to the five senses: sight, sound, touch, smell, or taste; a word or phrase that creates pictures in the reader's mind and that helps the reader's understanding of the poem

internal rhyme rhyme that occurs within a line (or lines) instead of at the end

limerick a five-line form of humorous verse with an *aabba* rhyme scheme
Ex: *There was an old man from Blackheath*
 Who sat on a set of false teeth,
 He cried with a start,
 "Oh, Lord, bless my heart!
 I've bitten myself underneath!"

line a single row of words appearing together on a line, considered as a unit

line break the end of a line of poetry; the place where a poet chooses to end a line

lyric a poem originally written for music and intended to be sung

metaphor an implied comparison of one object with another, with the first assuming the characteristics of the second; suggests a likeness or analogy between two unlike things but without using the words *like* or *as* (compare to *simile*)

Ex: *The world is a glass overflowing with water* (from "Ode to Enchanted Light" by Pablo Neruda)

meter the regular rhythmic pattern in a poem; the arrangement of beats or accents in a line of poetry designated by a pattern of stressed and unstressed syllables that helps establish the rhythm of a poem

mood the emotional aura or atmosphere created or conveyed by a poem, often determined by the words of a poem, its images, theme, etc.; synonymous or related to tone (e.g., friendly, solemn, wistful, thought-provoking, depressing)

near rhyme words that are *close* or that *almost* rhyme rather than being exact or precise in their rhyme pattern; sometimes called *off-rhyme* or *slant rhyme*

Ex: *park/work, busy/easy, barren/foreign*

octet an eight-line stanza

onomatopoeia use of words that imitate sounds and suggest their meaning.

Ex: *gargle, bark, sizzle, buzz*

personification to give an inanimate object, plant, or animal a human attribute or quality

Ex: *Because I could not stop for Death, He kindly stopped for me* (from "The Chariot" by Emily Dickinson)

prose ordinary speech or writing, as distinguished from verse; closely corresponds to patterns of everyday speech; when written, follows conventions of print, such as sentences, paragraphs, indenting, punctuation, etc.

quatrain a four-line stanza; may be unrhymed or have rhyme schemes such as *abab, aabb, abba,* or *abcb*

reader response theory synonymous with *Transactional Theory*; maintains that reader and literary text must *transact* in a fluid, active, reciprocal manner to construct meaning

repetition the repeated occurrence of sounds, words, phrases, or lines in a poem; adds rhythm and interest to a poem

rhyme the repetition of the same or similar vowel and consonant sounds, usually at the end of words

Ex: *blink/think* (identical rhyme) or *prove/love* (near rhyme)

rhyme scheme a consistent pattern of rhyme found in a stanza or a poem; this repetition of sounds is found most often at the end of lines but can also occur in the middle of one or more lines (this is called *internal rhyme*); rhyme scheme is designated or coded by lettering the lines according to their rhyming pattern: *abab, abcb, aabb,* and so on

rhyming (end-rhyme) poetry traditional poetry form in which rhyme occurs at the end of two or more lines

rhythm regularly repeated accents; the natural flow of stressed and unstressed syllables from word to word, line to line; synonymous with *cadence*

sextet a six-line stanza

simile the explicit comparison of one thing to another using the words *like* or *as* (compare to *metaphor*)

Ex: *as strong as an ox*

sonnet a 14-line poem concerned with a single thought or sentiment; written in iambic pentameter and following one of several rhyme schemes

stance a reader's predominant mindset, or what a reader focuses attention on, during a reading event; see *aesthetic stance, efferent stance,* and *reader response theory*

stanza grouping of lines arranged according to a fixed plan such as length or rhyme scheme; set apart by a blank line or other spacing to visually separate one stanza from another in a poem

stress emphasis on a particular syllable (see *accent*)

tercet or triplet a stanza of three lines that form a unit and usually rhyme

theme the general topic or subject of a poem

Ex: love, friendship, freedom, death, prejudice

tone the poet's underlying attitude, stance, or feeling conveyed in a poem (or other literary piece of work); sometimes used synonymously with *mood*

Ex: friendly, lighthearted, silly, somber, hostile, grief-stricken, irreverent, etc.

transaction the reciprocal and recursive interplay between reader and text, each influencing the other and both essential to the process of making meaning

Transactional Theory see *reader response theory*

Poems Cited in Text

Adoff, Arnold. "Five Ways to Scratch an Itch in the Center of My Back." In *Touch the Poem*. New York: Blue Sky Press, 2000.

Angelou, Maya. "Caged Bird." In *The Complete Collected Poems Of Maya Angelou*. New York: Random House, 1994.

Asch, Frank. "Lizards in Love." In *Cactus Poems*. Poems by Frank Asch, photographs by Ted Levin. San Diego: Harcourt Brace & Co., 1998.

Bodecker, N. M. "Sing Me a Song of Teapots and Trumpets." In *The Random House Book of Poetry for Children*. Selected by Jack Prelutsky. New York: Random House, 1983.

Brooks, Gwendolyn. "A Little Girl's Poem." In *This Place I Know: Poems of Comfort*. Selected by Georgia Heard. Cambridge, MA: Candlewick Press, 2002.

Carlisle, Andrea. "Emily Dickinson's To-Do List." In *I Feel a Little Jumpy Around You: A Book of Her Poems and His Poems Presented in Pairs*. Eds. Naomi Shihab Nye & Paul Janeczko. New York: Simon & Schuster Books for Young Readers, 1996.

Chosu. "Haiku." In *Light-Gathering Poems*. Ed. Liz Rosenberg. Translated by Harry Behn. New York: Henry Holt, 2000.

Coatsworth, Elizabeth. "Rain Poem." In *Sing a Song of Popcorn: Every Child's Book of Poems*. Selected by Beatrice Schenk de Regniers, Eva Moore, Mary Michaels White & Jan Carr. New York: Scholastic, 1988.

Collins, Billy. "Introduction to Poetry." In *Poetry 180: A Turning Back to Poetry*. Selected by Billy Collins. New York: Random House, 2003.

Cullen, Countee. "Incident." In *A Child's Anthology of Poetry*. Ed. Elizabeth Hauge Sword. New York: Scholastic, 1995.

cummings, e.e. "in Just-spring." In *Complete Poems 1913-1962*. New York: Harcourt Brace, 1972.

de Gasztold, Carmen Bernos. "The Prayer of the Little Ducks." In *Prayers from the Ark & the Creatures' Choir*. Translated by Rumer Godden. New York: Penguin Books, 1976.

Dickinson, Emily. "If I Can Stop One Heart from Breaking." In *Poetry for Young People: Emily Dickinson*. Ed. Frances Schoonmaker Bolin. New York: Sterling, 1994.

Dickinson, Emily. "A Narrow Fellow in the Grass." In *Poetry for Young People: Emily Dickinson*. Ed. Frances Schoonmaker Bolin. New York: Sterling, 1994.

Dickinson, Emily. "There Is No Frigate Like a Book." In *Poetry for Young People: Emily Dickinson*. Ed. Frances Schoonmaker Bolin. New York: Sterling, 1994.

Dickinson, Emily. "A Word Is Dead." In *Poetry for Young People: Emily Dickinson*. Ed. Frances Schoonmaker Bolin. New York: Sterling, 1994.

Dickinson, Emily. "The Chariot." In *Emily Dickinson Poems*. Ed. Johanna Brownell. Edison, NJ: Castle Books, 2002.

Driscoll, Louise. "Hold Fast to Your Dreams." In *A Child's Anthology of Poetry*. Ed. Elizabeth Hauge Sword. New York: Scholastic, 1995.

Farjeon, Eleanor. "Poetry." In *Inner Chimes: Poems on Poetry*. Selected by Bobbye S. Goldstein. Honesdale, PA: Wordsong/Boyds Mills Press, 1992.

Fisher, Lillian M. "Desert." In *My America: A Poetry Atlas of the United States*. Selected by Lee Bennett Hopkins. New York: Scholastic, 2000.

Frost, Robert. "Dust of Snow." In *A Child's Anthology of Poetry*. Ed. Elizabeth Hauge Sword. New York: Scholastic, 1995.

Frost, Robert. "The Road Not Taken." In *A Child's Anthology of Poetry*. Ed. Elizabeth Hauge Sword. New York: Scholastic, 1995.

George, Kristine O'Connell. "Autumn." In *Old Elm Speaks: Tree Poems*. New York: Clarion Books, 1998.

Greenfield, Eloise. "This Place." In *This Place I Know: Poems of Comfort*. Selected by Georgia Heard. Cambridge, MA: Candlewick Press, 2002.

Hoberman, Mary Ann. "Brother." In *Sing a Song of Popcorn: Every Child's Book of Poems*. Selected by Beatrice Schenk de Regniers, Eva Moore, Mary Michaels White & Jan Carr. New York: Scholastic, 1988.

Hoberman, Mary Ann. "May Fly." In *Seeing the Blue Between: Advice and Inspiration for Young Poets*. Compiled by Paul Janeczko. Cambridge, MA: Candlewick Press, 2002.

Hopkins, Lee Bennett. "Another." In *Been to Yesterdays: Poems of a Life*. Honesdale, PA: Wordsong/Boyds Mills Press, 1995.

Hubbell, Patricia. "Vermont Conversation." In *My America: A Poetry Atlas of the United States*. Selected by Lee Bennett Hopkins. New York: Scholastic, 2000.

Hughes, Langston. "April Rain Song." In *Sing a Song of Popcorn: Every Child's Book of Poems*. Selected by Beatrice Schenk de Regniers, Eva Moore, Mary Michaels White & Jan Carr. New York: Scholastic, 1988.

Hughes, Langston. "Mother to Son." In *The Dream Keeper and Other Poems*. New York: Knopf/Scholastic, 1994.

Hughes, Langston. "Reasons Why." In *The Dream Keeper and Other Poems*. New York: Knopf/Scholastic, 1994.

Johnston, Tony. "Cows." In *Once in the Country*. New York: G. P. Putnam's Sons, 1996.

Kinnell, Galway. "Blackberry Eating." In *The Norton Introduction to Poetry*, 6th Ed. Ed. J. Paul Hunter. New York: W.W. Norton, 1995.

Lewis, J. Patrick. "A Regular Riddle." In *Arithme-tickle: An Even Number of Odd Riddle-Rhymes*. San Diego: Harcourt, 2002.

Lowell, Amy. "Wind and Silver." In *Poetry U.S.A.* Ed. Paul Molloy. New York: Scholastic, 1968.

Medina, Tony. "I Do Not Like My Father Much." In *Love to Langston*. New York: Lee & Low Books, 2002.

Merriam, Eve. "Why I Did Not Reign." In *It Doesn't Always Have to Rhyme*. New York: Atheneum, 1964.

Merriam, Eve. "How to Eat a Poem." In *A Child's Anthology of Poetry*. Ed. Elizabeth Hauge Sword. New York: Scholastic, 1995.

Merriam, Eve. "Viper." In *Big, Bad, and a Little Bit Scary: Poems That Bite Back*. Illustrated by Wade Zahares. New York: Viking, 2001.

Moore, Rosalie. "Catalogue." In *A New Treasury of Children's Poetry*. Compiled by Joanna Cole. New York: Doubleday, 1984.

Nash, Ogden. "Adventures of Isabel." In *A New Treasury of Children's Poetry* Compiled by Joanna Cole. New York: Doubleday, 1984.

Neruda, Pablo. "What is it that upsets the volcanoes..." In *This Same Sky: A Collection of Poems from Around the World*. Selected by Naomi Shihab Nye. New York: Four Winds Press/Maxwell Macmillan, 1992.

Neruda, Pablo. "Ode to Enchanted Light." In *The Best Poems Ever: A Collection of Poetry's Greatest Voices*. Ed. Edric S. Mesmer. New York: Scholastic, 2001.

Oliver, Mary. "The poem is not the world." In *The Leaf and the Cloud: A Poem*. Cambridge, MA: Da Capo Press, 2000.

O'Neill, Mary. "Mimi's Fingers." In *Fingers Are Always Bringing Me News*. Garden City, NY: Doubleday, 1969.

O'Neill, Mary. "Feelings About Words." In *Inner Chimes: Poems on Poetry*. Selected by Bobbye S. Goldstein. Honesdale, PA: Wordsong/Boyds Mills Press, 1992.

Paul, Ann Whitford. "Sacajawea." In *All By Herself*. San Diego: Browndeer Press/Harcourt Brace, 1999.

Poe, Edgar Allen. "Annabel Lee." In *A Child's Anthology of Poetry*. Ed. Elizabeth Hauge Sword. New York: Scholastic, 1995.

Poe, Edgar Allan. "Eldorado." In *Poetry U.S.A.* Ed. Paul Molloy. New York: Scholastic, 1968.

Prelutsky, Jack. "Ballad of a Boneless Chicken." In *The New Kid on the Block*. New York: Greenwillow Books, 1984.

Prelutsky, Jack. "Bleezer's Ice Cream." In *The New Kid on the Block*. New York: Greenwillow Books, 1984.

Quenneville, Freda. "Mother's Biscuits." In *Reflections on a Gift of Watermelon Pickle and Other Modern Verse*. Eds. Stephen Dunning, Edward Lueders & Hugh Smith. New York: Lothrop, Lee & Shepard, [c.1966] 1967.

Rumi. "Let the beauty we love…" In *Light-Gathering Poems*. Ed. Liz Rosenberg. New York: Henry Holt, 2000.

Rylant, Cynthia. "Pet Rock." In *Waiting to Waltz: A Childhood*. Scarsdale, NY: Bradbury Press, 1984.

Sandburg, Carl. "Arithmetic." In *Sing a Song of Popcorn: Every Child's Book of Poems*. Selected by Beatrice Schenk de Regniers, Eva Moore, Mary Michaels White & Jan Carr. New York: Scholastic, 1988.

Sandburg, Carl. "Fog." In *A Child's Anthology of Poetry*. Ed. Elizabeth Hauge Sword. New York: Scholastic, 1995..

Schertle, Alice. "Consider Cow." In *How Now, Brown Cow?* San Diego: Browndeer Press, 1994.

Service, Robert. "The Cremation of Sam McGee." In *A Child's Anthology of Poetry*. Ed. Elizabeth Hauge Sword. New York: Scholastic, 1995.

Sexton, Anne. "Lobster." In *A Child's Anthology of Poetry*. Ed. Elizabeth Hauge Sword. New York: Scholastic, 1995..

Shakespeare, William. "Balcony Scene: Romeo and Juliet." In *Something Rich and Strange: A Treasury of Shakespeare's Verse*. Selected by Gina Pollinger. New York: Kingfisher, 1995.

Shakespeare, William. "Sonnet 18." In *Norton Anthology of Poetry*, 4th Ed. Margaret Ferguson. New York: W.W. Norton, 1996.

Siebert, Diane. "The farmer with his spirit strong…" In *Heartland*. New York: Thomas Y. Crowell, 1989.

Silverstein, Shel. "Crowded Tub." In *A Light in the Attic*. New York: HarperCollins, 1981.

Silverstein, Shel. "Smart." In *Where the Sidewalk Ends*. New York: HarperCollins, 1974.

Stafford, William. "Any Morning." In *What Have You Lost?* Selected by Naomi Shihab Nye. New York: HarperCollins, 1999.

Steagall, Red. "Hats Off to the Cowboy." In *Home on the Range: Cowboy Poetry*. Selected by Paul B. Janeczko. New York: Dial Books, 1997.

Thomas, Dylan. "Notes on the Art of Poetry." Web site: mbhs.bergtraum.k12.ny.us/cybereng/poetry/notes.html

Vallone, Antonio. "Statement" in *Roots and Flowers: Poets and Poems on Family*. Ed. Liz Rosenberg. New York: Henry Holt, 2001.

Viorst, Judith. "If I Were in Charge of the World." In *If I Were in Charge of the World and Other Worries: Poems for Children and Their Parents*. New York: Atheneum, 1981.

Viorst, Judith. "Don't Think." In *Sad Underwear and Other Complications: More Poems for Children and Their Parents*. New York: Atheneum, 1995.

Williams, William Carlos. "The Red Wheelbarrow." In *A Child's Anthology of Poetry*. Ed. Elizabeth Hauge Sword. New York: Scholastic, 1995.

Wolf, Allan. "Shy Silent Rivers." In *The Blood-Hungry Spleen and Other Poems About Our Parts*. Cambridge, MA: Candlewick Press, 2003.

Wolf, Allan. "Spit." In *The Blood-Hungry Spleen and Other Poems About Our Parts*. Cambridge, MA: Candlewick Press, 2003.

Wong, Janet. "Quilt." In *A Suitcase of Seaweed and Other Poems*. New York: Margaret K. McElderry, 1996.

Worth, Valerie. "Umbrella." In *Peacock and Other Poems*. New York: Farrar, Straus & Giroux, 2002.

Yolen, Jane. "The Fox and the Grapes" and "The Boy Who Cried Wolf." In *A Sip of Aesop*. New York: Blue Sky Press, 1995.

Yolen, Jane. "Grant Wood: American Gothic." In *Heart to Heart: New Poems Inspired by Twentieth-Century American Art*. Ed. Jan Greenberg. New York: Harry N. Abrams, 2001.

Professional Literature Cited in Text

Andrews, Richard. *The Problem with Poetry*. Philadelphia: Open University Press, 1991.

Atwell, Nancie. *In the Middle: Writing, Reading, and Learning with Adolescents*. Portsmouth, NH: Boynton/Cook, 1987.

Barry, Elaine. *Robert Frost on Writing*. New Brunswick, NJ: Rutgers University Press, 1973.

Cullinan, Bernice E., Scala, Marilyn C. & Schroder, Virginia C. *Three Voices: An Invitation to Poetry Across the Curriculum*. York, ME: Stenhouse, 1995.

Denman, Gregory A. *When You've Made It Your Own…: Teaching Poetry to Young People*. Portsmouth, NH: Heinemann, 1988.

Deutsch, Babette. *Poetry Handbook: A Dictionary of Terms*. New York: Funk & Wagnalls, 1974.

Doreski, Carole K. & Doreski, William. *How to Read and Interpret Poetry* (2nd ed.). New York: Prentice Hall, 1988.

Fletcher, Ralph. *Poetry Matters: Writing a Poem from the Inside Out*. New York: HarperTrophy, 2002.

Gaskins, Irene W., Rauch, Sharon & Gensemer, Eleanor [et al]. "Scaffolding the Development of Intelligence Among Children Who Are Delayed in Learning to Read." In Kathleen Hogan & Michael Pressley (Eds.), *Scaffolding Student Learning: Instructional Approaches and Issues* (43-73). Cambridge, MA: Brookline Books, 1997.

Haliburton, Margaret W. & Smith, Agnes G. *Teaching Poetry in the Grades*. Boston: Houghton Mifflin, 1911.

Heard, Georgia. *For the Good of the Earth and Sun*. Portsmouth, NH: Heinemann, 1989.

Heard, Georgia. *Awakening the Heart: Exploring Poetry in Elementary and Middle School*. Portsmouth, NH: Heinemann, 1999.

Holland, Kathleen E. & Shaw, Leslie A. "Dances Between Stances." In Kathleen E. Holland, Rachael A. Hungerford & Shirley B. Ernst (Eds.), *Journeying: Children Responding to Literature* (114-136). Portsmouth, NH: Heinemann, 1993.

hooks, bell. "Black is a Woman's Color." *Callaloo*, 12, no. 3 (1989).

Jong, Erica. *In Their Own Voices [sound recording]: A Century of Recorded Poetry*. Los Angeles: Rhino/Word Beat, 1996.

Lenz, Lisa. "Crossroads of Literacy and Orality: Reading Poetry Aloud." *Language Arts*, 69, no. 8 (December 1992): 597-603.

Lockward, Diane. "Poets on Teaching Poetry." *English Journal*, 83, no. 5 (September 1994): 65-70.

McClure, Amy A. *Sunrises and Songs: Reading and Writing Poetry in an Elementary Classroom*. Portsmouth, NH: Heinemann, 1990.

McClure, Amy A. & Zitlow, Connie S. "Not Just the Facts: Aesthetic Response in Elementary Content Area Studies." *Language Arts*, 68, no. 1 (January 1991): 27-33.

Mock, Jeff. *You Can Write Poetry*. Cincinnati, OH: Writer's Digest Books, 1998.

Murray, Donald M. *Crafting a Life in Essay, Story, Poem*. Portsmouth, NH: Boynton/Cook, 1996.

Myers, M. Priscilla. "Passion for Poetry." *Journal of Adolescent & Adult Literacy*, 41, no. 4 (December 1997/January 1998): 262-271.

Oldfather, Penny. "What Students Say About Motivating Experiences in a Whole Language Classroom." *The Reading Teacher*, 46, no. 8 (May 1993): 672-681.

Oliver, Mary. *A Poetry Handbook*. New York: Harcourt Brace, 1994.

Packard, William (Ed.). *The Craft of Poetry: Interviews from* The New York Quarterly. Garden City, NY: Doubleday, 1974.

Perfect, Kathy A. "A Case for Inviting More Aesthetic Response." *Ohio Reading Teacher*, 32, no. 1 (Fall 1997): 5-12.

Perfect, Kathy A. "Rhyme and Reason: Poetry for the Heart and Head." *The Reading Teacher*, 52, no. 7 (April 1999): 728-737.

The Power of the Word [videorecording]: *A Six-Part Series on Contemporary Poetry with Bill Moyers*. Produced by Public Affairs Television and David Grubin Productions. Princeton, NJ: Films for the Humanities & Sciences, 1994.

Rasinski, Timothy V. *The Fluent Reader: Oral Reading Strategies for Building Word Recognition, Fluency, and Comprehension*. New York: Scholastic, 2003.

Rasinski, Timothy V., & Padak, Nancy. *Effective Reading Strategies: Teaching Children Who Find Reading Difficult* (3rd Ed.). Columbus, OH: Merrill/Prentice Hall, 2004.

Rosenberg, Liz (Ed.). *Earth-Shattering Poems*. New York: Henry Holt, 1998.

Rosenblatt, Louise M. *The Reader, the Text, the Poem*. Carbondale, IL: Southern Illinois University Press, 1978.

Rosenblatt, Louise M. "'What Facts Does This Poem Teach You?'" *Language Arts*, 57, no. 4 (April 1980): 386-394.

Rosenblatt, Louise M. "The Literary Transaction: Evocation and Response." *Theory Into Practice*, 21, no. 4, (Fall 1982): 268-277.

Rosenblatt, Louise M. "Literature—S.O.S.!" *Language Arts*, 68, no. 6 (October 1991): 444-448.

Rosenblatt, Louise M. "The Transactional Theory: Against Dualism." *College English*, 55, no. 4 (April 1993): 377-386.

Rosenblatt, Louise M. *Literature as Exploration* (5th ed.). New York: The Modern Language Association, 1995.

Rozakis, Laurie E. *How to Interpret Poetry*. New York: Macmillan, 1998.

Stafford, William. *Writing the Australian Crawl: Views on the Writer's Vocation*. Ann Arbor, MI: The University of Michigan Press, 1978.

Vygotsky, Lev S. *Thought and Language*. Cambridge, MA: MIT Press, 1986.

Winokur, Jon. *Writers on Writing*. Philadelphia: Running Press, 1990.

Recommended Poetry Books and Anthologies

In addition to the books listed in the Bibliography, the following titles are recommended for use with intermediate and middle school students:

Adoff, Arnold. *The Basket Counts*. New York: Simon & Schuster, 2000.

Adoff, Arnold. *Eats*. New York: Mulberry Books, 1979.

Adoff, Arnold. *Love Letters*. New York: Scholastic, 1997.

Adoff, Arnold. *Touch the Poem*. New York: Blue Sky Press, 2000.

Adoff, Jaime. *The Song Shoots Out of My Mouth*. New York: Dutton Children's Books, 2002.

Anderson, Maggie & Hassler, David (Eds.). *Learning by Heart: Contemporary American Poetry About School*. Iowa City, IA: University of Iowa Press, 1999.

Berry, James (Selector). *Classic Poems to Read Aloud*. New York: Kingfisher, 1995.

Collins, Billy. *Sailing Alone Around the Room: New and Selected Poems*. New York: Random House, 2001.

Collins, Billy (Selector). *Poetry 180: A Turning Back to Poetry*. New York: Random House, 2003.

de Gasztold, Carmen Bernos. *Prayers from the Ark and Creatures' Choir*. Translated by Rumer Godden. New York: Penguin Books, 1976.

Duffy, Carol Ann (Ed.). *I Wouldn't Thank You for a Valentine: Poems for Young Feminists*. New York: Henry Holt, 1992.

Esbensen, Barbara Juster. *Echoes for the Eye: Poems to Celebrate Patterns in Nature*. New York: HarperCollins, 1996.

Fleischman, Paul. *Big Talk: Poems for Four Voices*. Cambridge, MA: Candlewick, 2000.

George, Kristine O'Connell. *Old Elm Speaks*. New York: Clarion Books, 1998.

Gordon, Ruth (Selector). *Pierced by a Ray of Sun: Poems About the Times We Feel Alone*. New York: HarperCollins, 1995.

Greenberg, Jan (Ed.). *Heart to Heart: New Poems Inspired by Twentieth-Century American Art*. New York: Harry N. Abrams, 2001.

Greenfield, Eloise. *Night on Neighborhood Street*. New York: Dial Books for Young Readers, 1991.

Hale, Glorya (Ed.). *Read-Aloud Poems for Young People*. New York: Black Dog & Leventhal, 1997.

Heard, Georgia (Selector). *This Place I Know: Poems of Comfort*. Cambridge, MA: Candlewick, 2002.

Hoberman, Mary Ann. *Fathers, Mothers, Sisters, Brothers: A Collection of Family Poems*. New York: Scholastic, 1991.

Holbrook, Sara. *Am I Naturally This Crazy?* Honesdale, PA: Wordsong/Boyds Mills Press, 1996.

Holbrook, Sara. *Which Way to the Dragon! Poems for the Coming-on-Strong*. Honesdale, PA: Boyds Mills Press, 1996.

Holbrook, Sara. *Wham! It's a Poetry Jam: Discovering Performance Poetry*. Honesdale, PA: Wordsong/Boyds Mills Press, 2002.

Hopkins, Lee Bennett (Selector). *Click, Rumble, Roar: Poems About Machines*. New York: Thomas Y. Crowell, 1987.

Hopkins, Lee Bennett. *Been to Yesterdays: Poems of a Life*. Honesdale, PA: Wordsong/Boyds Mills Press, 1995.

Hopkins, Lee Bennett (Selector). *My America: A Poetry Atlas of the United States*. New York: Scholastic, 2000.

Hughes, Langston. *The Dream Keeper and Other Poems*. New York: Knopf, 1994.

Janeczko, Paul (Selector). *Home on the Range: Cowboy Poetry*. New York, Dial Books, 1997.

Janeczko, Paul B. (Selector). *The Place My Words Are Looking For: What Poets Say About and Through Their Work*. New York: Simon & Schuster, 1990.

Janeczko, Paul B. *Scholastic Guides: How to Write Poetry*. New York: Scholastic, 1999.

Kennedy, X. J. and Dorothy M. Kennedy (Selectors). *Talking Like the Rain*. New York: Little Brown, 1992.

Kuskin, Karla. *The Sky Is Always in the Sky*. New York: HarperCollins, 1998.

Lewis, J. Patrick. *Arithme-tickle: An Even Number of Odd Rhymes*. San Diego: Harcourt, 2002.

Lewis, J. Patrick. *Doodle Dandies: Poems That Take Shape*. New York: Scholastic, 1998.

Medina, Tony. *Love to Langston*. New York: Lee & Low Books, 2002.

Mora, Pat. *This Big Sky*. New York: Scholastic, 1998.

Morrison, Lillian. *More Spice Than Sugar: Poems About Feisty Females*. Boston: Houghton Mifflin, 2001.

Myers, Walter Dean. *Brown Angels: An Album of Pictures and Verse*. New York: HarperCollins, 1993.

Nash, Ogden. *Custard and Company: Poems.* Boston: Little Brown, 1980.

Nye, Naomi Shihab. *Come with Me: Poems for a Journey.* New York: Greenwillow Books, 2000.

Nye, Naomi Shihab (Selector). *This Same Sky: A Collection of Poems from Around the World.* New York: Four Winds Press/Maxwell MacMillan, 1992.

Nye, Naomi Shihab and Paul Janeczko (Eds.). *I Feel a Little Jumpy Around You.* New York: Simon & Schuster Books for Young Readers, 1996.

Oliver, Mary. *The Leaf and the Cloud.* Cambridge, MA: Da Capo Press, 2000.

O'Neill, Mary. *Fingers Are Always Bringing Me News.* Garden City, NY: Doubleday, 1969.

O'Neill, Mary. *Hailstones and Halibut Bones: Adventures in Color.* New York: Doubleday, 1989.

Paul, Ann Whitford. *All By Herself.* San Diego: Browndeer Press/Harcourt Brace, 1999.

Pinsky, Robert and Maggie Dietz (Eds.). *Americans' Favorite Poems: The Favorite Poem Project Anthology.* New York: Norton, 1999.

Prelutsky, Jack. *New Kid on the Block.* New York: Greenwillow, 1984.

Prelutsky, Jack (Selector). *The Random House Book of Poetry for Children.* New York: Random House, 1983.

Rogasky, Barbara (Selector). *Winter Poems.* New York: Scholastic, 1994.

Rosen, Michael J. (Ed.). *Food Fight.* New York: Harcourt Brace, 1996.

Rosenberg, Liz (Ed.). *The Invisible Ladder: An Anthology of Contemporary American Poems for Young Readers.* New York: Henry Holt, 1996.

Rosenberg, Liz (Ed.). *Roots and Flowers: Poets and Poems on Family.* New York: Henry Holt, 2001.

Rylant, Cynthia. *Waiting to Waltz: A Childhood.* Scarsdale, NY: Bradbury, 1984.

Rylant, Cynthia. *Soda Jerk.* New York: Orchard Books, 1990.

Schenk de Regniers, Eva Moore, Mary Michaels White and Jan Car (Eds.) *Sing a Song of Popcorn: Every Child's Book of Poems.* New York: Scholastic, 1988.

Schertle, Alice. *Advice for a Frog.* New York: Lothrop, Lee, and Shepard, 1995.

Schmidt, Gary D. (Ed.). *Poetry for Young People: Robert Frost.* New York: Sterling, 1994.

Shields, Carol Diggory. *Lunch Money: And Other Poems About School.* New York: Penguin, 1995.

Siebert, Diane, *Heartland.* New York: Thomas Y. Crowell, 1989.

Sierra, Judy. *Antarctic Antics.* Orlando, FL: Harcourt Brace, 1998.

Silverstein, Shel. *A Light in the Attic.* New York: Harper & Row, 1981.

Silverstein, Shel. *Falling Up.* New York: HarperCollins, 1996.

Slier, Deborah (Ed.). *Make a Joyful Noise.* New York: Scholastic, 1991.

Sword, Elizabeth Hauge (Ed.). *A Child's Anthology of Poetry.* New York: Scholastic, 1995.

Vecchione, Patrice. *Truth and Lies: An Anthology of Poems.* New York: Henry Holt, 2001.

Volavkova, Hana (Ed.). *I Never Saw Another Butterfly: Children's Drawings and Poems from Terezin Concentration Camp 1942–1944.* New York: Schocken Books, 1993.

Westcott, Nadine B. (Selector). *Never Take a Pig to Lunch: And Other Poems About the Fun of Eating.* New York: Scholastic, 1994.

Wolf, Allan. *The Blood-Hungry Spleen and Other Poems About Our Parts.* New York: Candlewick Press, 2003.

Wong, Janet S. *A Suitcase of Seaweed.* New York: Margaret K. McElderry, 1996.

Wong, Janet S. *The Rainbow Hand: Poems About Mothers and Children.* New York: Simon & Schuster, 1999.

Wong, Janet S. *Night Garden: Poems from the World of Dreams.* New York: Simon & Schuster, 2000.

Wood, Nancy. *Spirit Walker.* New York: Doubleday, 1993.

Worth, Valerie. *All the Small Poems and Fourteen More.* New York: Farrar, Straus & Giroux, 1994.

Recommended Web Sites

Academy of American Poets: *www.poets.org/poets/*

Billy Collins: *www.bigsnap.com/billy.html*

Favorite Poem Project: *www.favoritepoem.org/*

IRA (International Reading Association): *www.reading.org*

Lesson Plan Index (IRA/NCTE Standards for the English Language Arts): *http://readwritethink.org/lesson/index.asp*

NCTE (National Council of Teachers of English): *www.ncte.org*

Poems on Poems: *http://mbhs.bergtraum.k12.ny.us/cybereng/poetry/index.html*

Poet Laureate Information (Poetry and Literature Center of the Library of Congress): *www.loc.gov/poetry/laureate.html*

Poetry - Awards, Contests, Poems, Terms: *www.libraryspot.com/poetry.htm*

The Poetry Center of Chicago: *www.poetrycenter.org*

Poetry Daily: *www.poems.com/*

Poetry 180: *www.loc.gov/poetry/180/p180-list.html*

Poetry Place—An Internet Hotlist on Poetry: *www.kn.pacbell.com/wired/fil/pages/listpoetrymr14.html*

Poetry Web sites: *www.poetrymagic.co.uk/resources.html*

September 11, 2001/The Response of Poetry: *www.geocities.com/poetryafterseptember112001/*

POETRY PROJECT

1. First, select a poem you like from one of our poetry books. The poem must be at least eight lines or more in length.

2. Now use your imagination to create a scene or environment for your poem. Use the words and images in the poem to give you ideas.

3. Make a poetry jar, poetry box, or poetry basket using your ideas. For example, a poem about the sea may include sand, seashells, seaweed, fish, etc. How you design or display it is up to you and your own imagination. Be creative!

4. Copy the selected poem in your best handwriting, or type it on a computer or typewriter. Make sure all words are spelled correctly and the lines look the way the poet intended. Include the poet's name on your copy.

5. Include your copy of the poem in the design of your box, jar, or basket. Display in a way that makes it easy to see and read.

6. Once your project is finished, ask yourself these questions and make any changes or additions you think it needs before handing it in:

   - *Is my project neatly done?*

   - *Is it interesting to look at?*

   - *Does my design match what the poem says or suggests?*

   - *Is my copy of the poem free of mistakes?*

   - *Did I remember to include the poet's name?*

   - *Is the poem attached and visible in the finished project?*

   - *Is my name clearly marked on my project?*

Due Date: _____

BIO POEM

LINE 1 (First name)

....

LINE 2 (Four adjectives that describe you)

....

LINE 3

Relative of . . . .

LINE 4 (3 items)

Lover of . . . .

LINE 5 (3 items)

Who feels . . . .

LINE 6 (3 items)

Who needs . . . .

LINE 7 (3 items)

Who gives . . . .

LINE 8 (3 items)

Who fears . . . .

LINE 9 (3 items)

Who would like to see . . . .

LINE 10

Resident of . . . .

LINE 11 (Last name)

....

Name _____ Date _____

"WHO AM I?" POEM

I'm _____ and _____ and _____ .
(3 adjectives)

I _____ and _____ and _____ .
(3 verbs)

I'm a _____ and _____ and _____ .
(3 nouns)

I sound like _____ ,

I feel like _____ ,

I move like _____ ,

and look like _____ .

I'm as _____ as a _____ ,

and _____ as a _____ .

I wait for _____ .

I long for _____ .

I hope for _____ .

I dream of _____ .

My name is _____ .

Credits

"Five Ways to Scratch an Itch in the Center of My Back" from TOUCH THE POEM by Arnold Adoff. Copyright © 2000 by Arnold Adoff. Reprinted by permission of Scholastic Inc.

"Lizards in Love" from CACTUS POEMS by Frank Asch. Copyright © 1998 by Frank Asch. Published by Harcourt Inc.

"Sing Me a Song of Teapots and Trumpets" is reprinted from HURRY, HURRY MARY DEAR AND OTHER NONSENSE POEMS by N.M. Boedecker. Copyright © 1976 by N. M. Boedecker. Published by Atheneum.

"A Little Girl's Poem" from VERY YOUNG POETS by Gwendolyn Brooks. Copyright © 1983 by the David Company, Chicago.

"Emily Dickinson's To-Do List" by Andrea Carlisle. Copyright © by Andrea Carlisle.

"Rain Poem" from POEMS by Elizabeth Coatworth. Copyright © 1957 by Macmillan Publishing Co., Inc.

"Introduction to Poetry" by Billy Collins. Copyright © 1988 by Billy Collins. Published by The University of Arkansas Press.

"Incident" from COLOR by Countee Cullen. Copyright © 1925 by Harper & Brothers, renewed 1953 by Ida M. Cullen.

"Poetry" from ELEANOR FARJEON'S POEMS FOR CHILDREN originally appeared in SING FOR YOUR SUPPER by Eleanor Farjeon. Copyright © 1938 by Eleanor Farjeon; renewed 1966 by Gervase Farjeon.

"Desert" by Lillian M. Fisher.

"The Prayer of the Little Ducks." From PRAYERS FROM THE ARK by Carmen Bernos de Gasztold, translated by Rumer Godden, copyright © 1962 renewed 1990 by Rumer Godden. Original copyright 1947, © 1955 by Editions du Cloitre. Used by permission of Viking Penguin, a division of Penguin Group (USA) Inc.

"Dust of Snow" from THE POETRY OF ROBERT FROST edited by Edward Connery Lathem. Copyright © 1944, 1951 by Robert Frost. Copyright © 1916, 1923, 1939, 1967, 1969, by Henry Holt and Company, Inc.

"Autumn" from OLD ELM SPEAKS: TREE POEMS by Kristine O'Connell George. Copyright © 1998 by Kristine O'Connell George. Published by Clarion Books.

"This Place" from UNDER THE SUNDAY TREE by Eloise Greenfield. Copyright © 1988 by Eloise Greenfield. Published by HarperCollins.

"Brother" by from HELLO AND GOOD-BY by Mary Ann Hoberman. Copyright © 1959 by Mary Ann Hoberman. Published by Harcourt Inc.

"May Fly" is reprinted from THE LLAMA WHO HAD NO PAJAMA by Mary Ann Hoberman. Copyright © 1998 by Mary Ann Hoberman. Published by Harcourt Inc.

"Another" from BEEN TO YESTERDAYS by Lee Bennett Hopkins. Copyright © 1995 by Lee Bennett Hopkins. Published by Word Song/Boyds Mills Press.

"Vermont Conversation" by Patricia Hubbell.

"Mother to Son" "April Rain Song" and 2 lines from "Reasons Why" by Langston Hughes From THE COLLECTED POEMS OF LANGSTON HUGHES by Langston Hughes. Copyright © 1994 by Langston Hughes. Reprinted by permission of Alfred A. Knopf, a division of Random House, Inc.

"Cows" from ONCE IN THE COUNTRY by Tony Johnston. Copyright © 1996 by Tony Johnston. Published by G.P Putnam's Sons.

"A Regular Riddle" from ARITHME-TICKLE: AN EVEN NUMBER OF ODD RHYMES by J. Patrick Lewis. Copyright © 2002 by J. Patrick Lewis. Published by Harcourt Inc.

"Wind and Silver" by Amy Lowell. Published by Houghton Mifflin Co.

"I Do Not Like My Father Much" from LOVE TO LANGSTON by Tony Medina. Copyright © 2002 by Tony Medina. Published by Lee and Low Books.

"Why I Did Not Reign" by Eve Merriam. From IT DOESN'T ALWAYS HAVE TO RHYME by Eve Merriam. Copyright © 1964, 1992 by Eve Merriam. Used by permission of Marian Reiner.

"Viper" from HALLOWEEN A B C by Eve Merriam. Copyright © 1987 by Eve Merriam. Reprinted by permission of Marian Reiner.

"The poem is not the world" by Mary Oliver from THE LEAF AND THE CLOUD. Copyright © 2000 by Mary Oliver. Published by Da Capo Press.

"Feelings About Words" from WORDS WORDS WORDS by Mary O'Neill. Copyright © 1966 by Mary O'Neill. Published by Doubleday, a division of Bantam Doubleday Dell Publishing Group, Inc.

"Mimi's Fingers" from FINGERS ARE ALWAYS BRINGING ME NEWS by Mary O'Neill. Copyright © 1969 by Mary O'Neill. Published by Doubleday.

"Ode to Enchanted Light" from ODES TO OPPOSITES by Pablo Neruda. Copyright © 1995 by Pablo Neruda and Fundacion Pablo Neruda (Odes in Spanish); Copyright © 1995 by Ken Krabbenhoft (Odes in English). Published by Little, Brown and Co.

"What is it that upsets the volcanoes" by Pablo Neruda.

"Bleezer's Ice Cream" from THE NEW KID ON THE BLOCK by Jack Prelutsky. Copyright © 1984 by Jack Prelutsky. Published by HarperCollins.

"Mother's Biscuits" by Freda Quenneville. Copyright © by Freda Quenneville. Published by Michigan State University Press.

"Consider Cow" from HOW NOW BROWN COW? by Alice Shertle. Copyright © 1994 by Alice Shertle. Published by Harcourt, Inc.

"Any Morning" by William Stafford. Copyright © 1993 by William Stafford. First appeared in Ohio Review, 50th Volume.

"Hats Off to the Cowboy" by Red Steagall. Copyright © 1989 by Texas Red Songs.

"Arithmetic" by Carl Sandburg. From THE COMPLETE POEMS OF CARL SANDBURG. Copyright © 1970, 1969 by Lilian

Steichen Sandburg, Trustee, reprinted by permission of Harcourt, Inc.

"The farmer with his spirit strong" from HEARTLAND by Diane Siebert. Copyright © 1989 by Diane Siebert. Published by HarperCollins.

"Don't Think" by Judith Viorst. Reprinted with permission of Atheneum Books for Young Readers, an imprint of Simon & Schuster Children's Publishing Division, from SAD UNDERWEAR AND OTHER COMPLICATIONS by Judith Viorst. Text copyright © 1995 by Judith Viorst. All rights reserved.

"If I Were in Charge of the World" from IF I WERE IN CHARGE OF THE WORLD AND OTHER WORRIES by Judith Viorst. Copyright © 1981 by Judith Viorst. Published by Atheneum.

"Sacajawea" from ALL BY HERSELF by Ann Whitford Paul. Copyright © 1999 by Ann Whitford Paul. Published by Harcourt Inc.

"The Red Wheelbarrow" from COLLECTED POEMS 1909-1939, VOLUME 1 by William Carlos Williams. Copyright 1938 by New Directions Publishing Corporation.

"Spit" and "Shy Silent Rivers" from THE BLOOD-HUNGRY SPLEEN AND OTHER POEMS ABOUT OUR PARTS by Allan Wolf. Copyright © 2003 by Allan Wolf. Published by Candlewick Press.

"Quilt" from A SUITCASE OF SEAWEED AND OTHER POEMS by Janet Wong. Published by Margaret K. McElderry Books.

"Umbrella" from PEACOCK AND OTHER POEMS by Valerie Worth. Copyright © 2002 by Valerie Worth. Published by Farrar Straus & Giroux.

"Grant Wood: American Gothic" by Jane Yolen from HEART TO HEART: NEW POEMS INSPIRED BY TWENTIETH-CENTURY AMERICAN ART edited by Jan Greenburg. Copyright © 2001 by Harry N. Abrams, Inc.

2 excerpts from A SIP OF AESOP by Jane Yolen. Copyright © 1995 by Jane Yolen. Reprinted by permission of Scholastic Inc.